WILDFLOWERS
AND
BROKEN GODS

A Year in Greece

Linda Syverson

Backstage Pass Publishing
Victoria, TX

For information, please contact:
Backstage Pass Publishing
P.O. Box 695
Victoria TX 77902

Author contact:
lindasyverson@yahoo.com

Cover Art by Tony Szatkowski.

Editing and Interior Formatting by Matt Syverson.

Special thanks to my son and editor, Matt, for believing in me and going the extra mile. I'm very grateful to my husband, Al, and my daughter, Tamara, for their endless love, support, and encouragement. Thanks to Tony for lending his talent, expertise, and kind assistance to this project.

Printed by Lightning Source in the U.S. and U.K.
Also available for Kindle.

ISBN: 978-0-9854895-3-3

Dedicated to my harnessed child.
Without his encouragement,
our story would not have
been written.

MACEDONIA

BULGARIA

ALBANIA

TURKEY

TURKEY

GREECE

AEGEAN SEA

Nafpaktos

Araxos · Patras

Kato Achaia

Olympia

Corinth

Athens

IONIAN SEA

PELOPONNESE

SEA OF CRETE

Crete

MEDITERRANEAN SEA

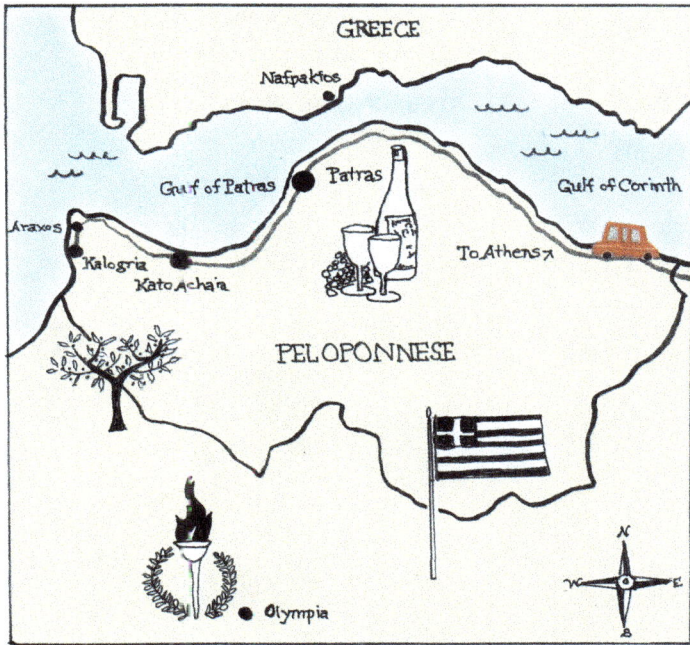

This is a true story.

CONTENTS

PLAY LIST

The following songs are listed throughout our story at 'cue the music'. For a complete sensory experience, I recommend watching the original musical performances or listening to the original recordings on You Tube.

"Leaving on a Jet Plane"
Peter, Paul, and Mary

"I Say a Little Prayer"
Dionne Warwick

"The Letter"
The Box Tops

"A Beautiful Morning"
The Rascals

"Happy Together"
The Turtles

"You Ain't Goin' Nowhere"
The Byrds

"Picture Book"
The Kinks

"Lookin' Out My Back Door"
Creedence Clearwater Revival

"Turn! Turn! Turn!"
The Byrds

"Find the Cost of Freedom"
Crosby, Stills, Nash, and Young

"Crystal Blue Persuasion"
Tommy James and the Shondells

"Lucy in the Sky with Diamonds"
The Beatles

"So Far Away"
Carole King

"Peace Train"
Cat Stevens

"I Can See Clearly Now"
Johnny Nash

"Aquarius/Let the Sunshine In"
The 5th Dimension

"Grazin' in the Grass"
The Friends of Distinction

"Behind Blue Eyes"
The Who

"Stairway to Heaven"
Led Zeppelin

"You Showed Me"
The Turtles

"Here Comes the Sun"
The Beatles

"Magic Carpet Ride"
Steppenwolf

"For Your Love"
The Yardbirds

"Pictures of Matchstick Men"
Status Quo

"Your Song"
Elton John

"For What It's Worth"
Buffalo Springfield

"On the Road Again"
Canned Heat

"Fortunate Son"
Creedence Clearwater Revival

"Heart Full of Soul"
The Yardbirds

"Heart of Gold"
Neil Young

"More Love"
Smokey Robinson and the Miracles

"My Blue Heaven"
Fats Antoine Domino

"All Summer Long"
The Beach Boys

"Let's Live for Today"
The Grass Roots

"If You Could Read My Mind"
Gordon Lightfoot

"Day after Day"
Badfinger

"Homeward Bound"
Simon and Garfunkel

"What the World Needs Now"
Jackie DeShannon

"Two of Us (On Our Way Home)"
The Beatles

"Spirit in the Sky"
Norman Greenbaum

Ballad of a Bohemian Dream

American writer Gelett Burgess described the bohemian life:

"To take the world as one finds it, the bad with the good, making the best of the present moment—to laugh at Fortune alike whether she be generous or unkind—to spend freely when one has money, and to hope gaily when one has none—to fleet the time carelessly, living for love . . . there are no roads in all Bohemia! One must choose and find one's own path, be one's own self, live one's own life."

Ω Ω Ω

Right in the middle of our ordinary lives, my family and I were given an opportunity to take another path. We traveled to the other side of the world, to Greece, to live for one year in a faraway rural village. We skipped out on our *Leave it to Beaver* existence and our American way of life. Our year in Greece changed us forever. It gave us a deep appreciation of the diverse lifestyles of people spread over the globe. It taught us another way to live.

A small band of Americans formed an expatriate community there, which was our answer to the Paris Left Bank of the 1920s. We found we could live quite well and happily with little money and few possessions, just as Hemingway and Picasso had done before us.

Our food and wine were shared. We received our car as a gift and gave it to another wanderer when we were finished with it. Our rustic home had no television and little music except the melodies in our own heads. The year was filled with comedy and tragedy just as life always is. This is our story.

1 – THE LONG AND WINDING ROAD

The shrill ring of a black rotary-dial telephone woke me from my restless sleep at 2:00 a.m. My head popped up from my crumpled pillow, and I was instantly alert. I sprinted through the house to the kitchen wall phone in the dark.

I had not slept well for several nights, tossing and turning in the tangled sheets, anticipating a call from my husband, Al. Was I dreaming?

We had not spoken to each other for three long months. Air mail letters were our only means of communication during this separation, and they took three weeks to be delivered.

"Hello?" I said hopefully, my voice muffled by sleep.

"Baby!!! I love you!"

I was elated to hear my husband's voice again, although he sounded very far away. There was a lot to catch up on, but the connection was bad, so the call was short and to the point.

"I love you, too. Where in the world are you?"

"I'm in Athens. I've been sittin' here for hours waiting for this call to go through to you. I've found us a house to rent for one year in Kato. It's the nicest house in town."

Kato, Achaia, a remote village on the Peloponnese, the southern peninsula of Greece, would be our new home town.

"I'll start packing right now. I thought I'd die waiting to hear from you." Static crackled along the phone line reaching all the way from Greece to the middle of America.

"I love you and my munchkins dearly . . ." Another crackle and he was gone.

And so our great adventure began . . .

Ω Ω Ω

WILD 2 FLOWERS

Looking back from the perspective of my sixty-fourth year, I see my time in Greece was the greatest exploit of my life. The year was 1971. The violent and anti-establishment Sixties had turned us all into borderline hippies. Even military men were no longer in favor of the Vietnam War.

Al, like most of his fellow airmen, had joined the Air Force to avoid the draft. Now he had been stationed at what the military termed a 'remote isolated detachment' in Greece, called Araxos, to work in a tiny tin-roofed shack as a radio operator.

I had seen firsthand the negative effects of year-long separations on other Air Force families I knew. Wives who had all the responsibilities of being the head of the household thrust upon them found it hard to relinquish control when their husbands came home. Subsequent power struggles often could not be resolved, and the couples divorced.

The Women's Liberation Movement was beginning to have an effect on traditional gender roles in American society in the early Seventies. The male-dominated military culture was one of the last battles for the bra burners in their quest for equality of the sexes. We always heard the saying, 'If the Air Force wanted you to have a wife, they would have issued you one.'

I saw my young children changing daily. A year would be too long for them to be apart from their father, and he would miss too many firsts in their lives. I was determined the kids and I would not be left behind, no matter what hardships I might have to endure living in a tiny village on foreign soil.

When I contemplate the woman I was in 1971, I don't know why I wasn't frightened by the prospect of traveling around the world to a strange place with an infant in my arms and a toddler at my side. The primal instinct to keep my family together drove me on. I didn't feel an iota of fear or apprehension.

Up to that point in my life, the biggest risk I had taken was riding shotgun in my girlfriend's Pontiac Bonneville. Looking back, I see that was way too much horsepower for an unseasoned high school girl to handle.

Greek philosopher Socrates said, "The only true wisdom is in knowing you know nothing."

I was too naïve to realize what I didn't know. Having been raised in the rarefied air of small town middle America, I had always felt protected and safe. Talk about innocents abroad.

At 2:15 a.m. I began packing – with uncommon thought and care. I would only be allowed to check one large suitcase on our flight. The crucial contents had to suffice for the next year for me, my one-year-old son, Matthew, and my infant daughter, Tamara. I tried to visualize what we would need as I packed their tiny clothes.

I knew I could buy clothing in Greece, but it was essential to make sure we had the things we would need on the trip and immediately after we arrived. I was allowed a good sized carry-on diaper bag, which I stocked with bottles of pre-measured powdered milk, jars of baby food, baby cereal, zwieback teething biscuits, and as many disposable diapers as would fit. We would have to rely on the stewardesses for warm water during the long flight. I had purchased a child-sized harness and leash for Matt. I couldn't stand the thought of losing him in the crowd at bustling John F. Kennedy International Airport in New York.

Over the previous couple months, the children and I had begun to feel like human pincushions. We needed many inoculations before we would be allowed to travel to Europe. Tammy was lucky. Since she was only a few months old, she didn't have to take all the shots. The worst vaccination we endured was for typhoid fever, which caused both Matt and me to have feverish swollen lumps on our arms that took several days to subside.

After scrimping and saving religiously, I had the money to

pay for the round-trip tickets, which the Air Force insisted upon, along with a little extra in Traveler's Checks. The Air Force didn't like airmen's families going to remote isolated locations, and they certainly didn't want them stranded there with no ticket home if a war or some catastrophe broke out.

The stubborn independent streak I've always had made me certain that the children and I were going to Greece, come hell or high water. Few credit cards were being used in 1971. I didn't have one, so cash or Traveler's Checks were my only choices.

With the bags all packed, I woke the kids and got them dressed and fed. Then we hit the road to the Will Rogers World Airport in Oklahoma City. My parents went along to see us off and take our car back to their house. We drove for two and a half hours.

We parked, and our little clan made its way to the check-in counter inside the airport. My dad carried our big suitcase. I was perturbed when I found the tickets would cost more than the price I had been quoted – the first hint of adversity on our trip to the other side of the world.

"Dad, do you have any cash on you? They say the tickets are $157.00 more than they told me two days ago."

I borrowed the money from my dad and paid for the tickets. Mine was a full fare, Matt's was a half fare, and Tammy's was free, based on the assumption she would ride in my lap the whole way. Flying was much more expensive then than now. Today we could fly to Europe for a fraction of what I paid in 1971.

After hugs and kisses that would have to last a whole year were exchanged, we left Mom and Dad at the gate.

Cue the music:
"Leaving on a Jet Plane"
Peter, Paul, & Mary

The late Sixties and early Seventies were the heyday of commercial air travel. Flying then was luxurious compared to the sardine-like conditions we endure today.

My two tiny companions and I ascended the rolling stairway attached to the side of the jet. The stewardesses greeted us warmly. Back then, all the flight attendants looked like models, wearing trendy little suits and hats. At that time, attendants had to meet strict height and weight requirements. The airlines actually used the stewardesses' attractiveness as a selling feature in advertising. A popular campaign used the slogan, 'I'm Barbara! Fly me to Orlando'. This was obviously before sexism became an issue.

The capable 'stews' were at hand to help us get settled into our wide leather seats. We rode in comfort. Flying then was much plusher than traveling by car. Our plane taxied to the runway. Matt was belted into his seat next to me, and Tammy rode on my lap. In a few moments, the jet accelerated and lifted off.

We relaxed when the pilot spoke soothingly over the intercom, and after a few minutes he told us we could release our seat belts. The seat next to me was empty, so I was able to lay Tammy down there. After a while, I got warm water for her bottle. She showed mild disapproval of the powdered milk, but overall the flight was pleasant. As the astronauts say, 'All systems go'. Off we went into the wild blue yonder with our passport, shot records, and our diaper bag.

Our schedule would be tight. We were to land at LaGuardia Airport, where a prearranged Red Cross driver would meet us and transport us across New York City to John F. Kennedy International Airport. It was crucial that we catch our connecting flight, and we had little time to spare.

Only one international flight departed for Athens that day. If we missed our flight, we would be stuck in the airport overnight. That disturbing thought gave me a queasy feeling in the pit of my stomach. I tried not to dwell on it. I knew if I started worrying about the 'what ifs' it would be like unraveling yarn from a sweater. I would end up with a big pile of apprehension at my feet. I tried to stay positive, which is my natural inclination.

About an hour before our scheduled landing at LaGuardia, the plane began to experience turbulence. The bumpy air amplified into a full scale thunderstorm with lightning slicing across the darkened sky. The plane bucked like a bronc in a rodeo back home.

"Ladies and Gentlemen, this storm has things a little backed up at LaGuardia. Our arrival will be temporarily delayed. We've been instructed to stack up and circle until things calm down. I'll keep you posted," the soft-spoken captain said over the intercom. The captain's practiced calm demeanor was meant to make us feel better.

I was jittery and jumpy from the roller coaster ride we were having, but even more so from the thought we might miss our connection. Fortunately, the kids remained calm and unconcerned, behaving like seasoned travelers.

One hour and then another half-hour slowly passed. Worry crept around my mind like a spider building a web.

At last the captain got clearance to land, even though it was still stormy. The landing was bumpy and jerky. By the time we came to a complete stop, my nerves were shot.

Relieved to be on solid ground, I hooked up Matt's harness and leash. I quickly grabbed Tammy and our carry-on bag. We took our place in line to descend the rolling stairway, which had been pushed up to the door of the jet. Rain was still coming down hard. We gingerly made our way down the steep stairs, but still had fifty yards to walk across the tarmac in the deluge. By the time we got inside, we looked like we had all just been baptized. My shoes squeaked with each step I took.

I immediately scanned the terminal, searching for the Red Cross driver. I spotted the short, disheveled man wearing a wrinkled trench coat and holding a sign with my name on it. He looked like a knight in shining armor to me. I felt like we had been rescued.

The driver retrieved our lone piece of luggage from the baggage claim and helped us into his beat-up station wagon. He took off for JFK, speeding when he could, even though it was still raining hard. He knew we were in danger of missing our connecting flight.

We reached Kennedy International in record time. The wet pavement reflected the head lights as we came to an abrupt stop in front of the Trans World Airline Terminal.

"I can never thank you enough for helping us like this. We wouldn't have made it without you," I said as I grasped my hero's hand.

"Glad to help, lady. It's what we do," he replied humbly.

We left him there at the curb, and Matt, Tammy, and I entered the double doors of the terminal. A sea of people of many races and creeds stood before us.

The room personified the melting pot of America. We were engulfed in the most crowded place this country girl had ever been. It was even more jam-packed than the state fair back home. I silently thanked the Lord for Matt's harness and leash, even though they did draw some strange looks from other travelers.

The three of us jostled our way through the crush of people, and I heard many unrecognizable languages being spoken. This melting pot was more like a hearty stew. We were all in this together, but we each retained our individual cultural influences.

I struggled, elbow to elbow, carrying Tammy and the luggage through the throng of globe-trotters crowded around us.

Matt walked close beside me on his leash. It took every ounce of my strength to carry the weight and press through the horde of travelers. My eyes searched for direction signs all along our path.

Mothers of toddlers attain amazing arm strength from lifting them enumerable times each day. A personal trainer can't match the tone and muscles this process builds in even the skinniest of arms. This, and my gritty determination had to be what enabled me to push forward. In my head, I kept saying, *I can do this . . . I can do this.*

At last, we made our way to the Trans World Airline counter. I showed our tickets and checked our large suitcase. The three of us were rushed to the gate on a tram.

Most of the passengers were already aboard, but only about half the seats were taken. There was a full row of available seats over the wing where we could stretch out and relax. I raised the armrests, so it was more like a couch. When the kids were settled, I sank into my leather chair with great relief. I sat silently and inhaled several deep breaths.

A clear feminine voice coming over the intercom interrupted the quiet. "The departure of the flight to Athens will be delayed."

I sat watching the rain stream down the window for about two hours. The storm finally subsided, and our plane was cleared for departure.

Most of the passengers looked like business men. I was hoping everyone would settle down for a quiet night while our jet circumnavigated the globe, but that was not to be.

The party began as soon as the seat belt sign went off. The stewardesses hovered around the executives, laughing and serving drinks. They showed little interest in providing anything for my family. I had difficulty drawing the attendants' attention away from the business men and their socializing, but grudgingly they gave us pillows, blankets, and warm water. The kids quieted down, and I tried to rest.

I was still wide awake when the plane crested the horizon, and I witnessed the astonishing sunrise created by our movement around the earth. It was an unforgettable moment. Relief and happiness washed over me, and I thought to myself, *At least our family is all on the same side of the planet now.*

Cue the music:
"I Say a Little Prayer"
Dionne Warwick

2 – LIKE A ROLLING STONE

I dozed off and caught a nap while Matt and Tammy slept next to me. After several hours, the plane touched down in Portugal, our first stop in Europe. At that time all the English speaking pilots, crew members, and flight attendants disembarked. Their replacements spoke only Spanish, a language I did not speak. From then on, I had to try to convey our needs with crude charade performances, which they seemed to find entertaining.

I later learned that most Europeans speak two or three languages and look down on Americans for being lax in that department. They consider us a little self-absorbed.

With the well-rested new crew at their stations, the plane lifted off the tarmac, and we were airborne once more.

The next stop was Madrid, Spain. I looked out the window and scanned the area for a landmark I might commit to memory, but saw only a flat, dusty, barren landscape. Before long, we were in the air again.

The airline food served to us while we flew over Europe was a far cry from the three squares we were used to. The meals were what Americans would call a light snack. The offerings were primarily cheese and crackers, and the cheese was stinky and runny to boot. I only weighed 110 pounds at that time, and I was not what you would call a big eater. I was, however, a meat eater, raised in cattle country. Visions of steaks and hamburgers danced through my head. My stomach rumbled. This trip was taking so long, and I was beginning to feel acutely underfed. I was afraid I would pounce on the next edible scrap I saw and embarrass myself.

Little did I know that I was going to a place where meat was treated more like a condiment than the main course.

The flight made an unscheduled stop in Rome, Italy. I was extremely alarmed when two uniformed officials boarded our jet and came directly to my seat. The men motioned for me and the children to deplane. They pulled on my arm, speaking Italian, which of course I didn't understand. I waved our passport in front of them, but they barely glanced at it.

The kids and I were all on the same passport in a photo taken on an extremely hot day in western Oklahoma. In the picture, Matt was shirtless and was sucking his thumb, and Tammy looked disgruntled. I was trying to hold both of them on my lap and smile. Maybe the uniformed men didn't recognize us.

The children and I were forced to leave our seats, descend the rolling stairs, and cross the tarmac. Our little tribe of nomads, accompanied by the two men, stood inside the terminal looking out a large plate glass window toward our plane. How would I explain to Al that we had been thrown off the plane in the wrong country? So close, but yet so far. We were just one country away from Greece.

A helpful gentleman tried to come to our aid. He struggled to explain to me in broken English why we had been forced to leave the plane.

"It is incest."

My eyes flew open wide. "It's what?" I said, my voice going up an octave.

He made crawling and flying motions with his fingers. "Bugs!"

"Oh, you mean insects."

Eventually, I understood it was to ensure the children's safety that we had been removed from our seats. Some type of flying insect was infesting the citrus fruit trees in Italy, and planes could not even fly over the country without landing to be fumigated. While the three of us waited inside the airport with the two officials, several other uniformed men sprayed insecticide around the other passengers and in the lower compartments of the jet with antique-looking outmoded pump sprayers.

The other passengers showed no ill effects when we were allowed to return to our seats. Their grins indicated they were happy we were back on board.

Cue the music:
"The Letter"
The Box Tops

In the air once more, we were ready for this expedition to end. I felt like I had been to a three day slumber party. I was surviving on a couple of cat naps and very little to eat since we left Oklahoma.

After a short while, we landed in Athens. Terra firma, at last. We had traveled almost twenty-four hours, and my little globe-trotters had logged more air miles than most people do in a lifetime. I felt like kissing the ground.

Our single carefully packed suitcase did not arrive with us, but came on the next flight from New York the following day. The customs inspectors, who are not known for smiling about anything, were amused by our passport picture. One of the agents rifled through our meager belongings in the diaper bag, stamped our passport, and allowed us to pass into the Athens International Airport Terminal.

Dozens of uniformed soldiers carrying guns were standing throughout the facility. Their eyes visually frisked each person who passed by, including us.

Most Americans were pretty oblivious to terrorism before 9/11/01, but Europe and the Middle East have endured acts of terrorism for decades. Athens had been the victim of several violent incidents. Skyjacking was the terrorist's favorite technique to gain control over a plane load of innocents to be held hostage. The threat hadn't even crossed my mind until I saw the armed soldiers. Now I was alarmed.

I stood at the side of the large, high-ceilinged room, holding Tammy with Matt on his leash, my eyes searching frantically for my husband.

Growing up in the center of the USA, I was used to being around people of every color from pale pink with freckles to the blackest black. I noticed right away that everyone in the airport, except me and my children, had dark hair, ebony eyes, and olive-toned skin. We looked terribly out of place. It was as if we were on a stage with a spot light aimed at us. I tried unsuccessfully to blend in.

After a half hour, my darling husband, Al, appeared. My heart jumped when I saw him. He embraced all three of us at once and twirled us around. *Everything will be alright now*, I thought.

I hadn't realized I'd been holding my tense shoulders up around my ears. I felt such joy and relief seeing Al, and I relaxed for the first time in several hours. Whatever lay ahead, we could handle it together.

I learned that Al had been expecting our plane to arrive on the previous day. He had waited several hours at the airport, but couldn't find out anything about our delay. I'm sure skyjacking crossed his mind. He returned by chance at the correct time on the day of our arrival. Now you know why I believe in guardian angels.

We piled into a taxi to travel to the Hotel Kreoli, a favorite lodging of the American Air Force travelers. Chatting and playing with the kids, we were reacquainting ourselves after our long separation. It was wonderful to be together again.

An attentive bellboy showed us to our room. The accommodations were elegant in the spare European fashion. The floors were veined marble, and the crisp linens were sumptuous. The contrast to the motel rooms we had occupied back in the States was striking. I felt like a pampered jet-setter.

After taking in the luxuriant room and bath, we stepped onto the balcony outside to survey the city and the sea beyond. Below us grew an enormous red geranium in a huge urn on the hotel's manicured lawn. The panorama was a beautiful sight to behold.

A peaceful night's rest helped us get our land legs. For months, Tammy had been a fretful baby. Night after night, I had walked the floor with her, trying to soothe her. From our first night in Athens on, she slept serenely. Our family was reunited, and harmony was restored.

Cue the music:
"A Beautiful Morning"
The Rascals

The next morning was spent sightseeing and trying local food. Near the hotel, we lunched on the largest shrimp I have ever seen. They were six inches long, and the waiter called them 'prawns'. A Greek salad and fried potatoes accompanied the delicious crustaceans.

In downtown Athens, we did a 'drive by' rubbernecking tour of the Parthenon, the Greek Parliament, and the streets around the Acropolis.

The Acropolis is a magnificent mesa in the center of the ancient section of Athens known as the *agora*. *Acro* means 'the top' and *polis* means 'city'. The early citizens saw the hill with steep sides and a flat top as the most astounding landmark in the area and named it 'the top of the city'.

I was awestruck the first time I looked up and saw the Parthenon on top of the butte. The structure was built between 447 and 438 BC as a temple to honor the goddess, Athena, the mythical guardian of Athens.

I'd seen pictures of it in my school books, but the real thing left me almost speechless. The base is 101 feet by 228 feet, and it is nearly five stories tall, but it looks much taller because it sits atop the 512-foot-high limestone mesa.

"I had no idea . . . how huge . . . this would be. I'm impressed," I stammered.

"Just think," Al said. "They built all this without giant cranes or bulldozers."

"Amazing."

Most of the cabs we rode in were Mercedes, but traffic regulations didn't seem to exist. All five lanes were full of cars and trucks, lined up bumper to bumper. Everyone was going exceptionally fast and changing lanes spontaneously. I found myself holding my breath.

In the afternoon, a taxi took us back to the airport to fetch the overdue suitcase. Ready to see our new home, we then went back to the hotel to check out. We knew we would be returning to Athens before long.

Al had ridden one way from Kato with a fellow airman, one of a few Americans who owned a vehicle. The airmen's custom was to hand down their car to a new arrival when their tour of duty at Araxos Detachment was over. The same procedure was used for household goods. No money changed hands in these transactions. Al had furnished our new house primarily by this method, and he hoped to get his international driver's license and a car for us soon.

The money exchange rate was favorable for Americans. It remained a stable thirty drachmas to one American dollar for the entire year we were in Greece. We could live pretty well on an airman's pay.

For the trip back to our new home, Al arranged for a taxi to drive us all the way from Athens to Kato, a distance of about 242 kilometers.

Greece, like most of the world, was on the metric system. That distance was about 150 American miles. The trip would be much more comfortable and much faster than riding the train or a crowded bus.

That cab ride would be the last bit of luxury we would experience for quite a while.

The prearranged taxi, driven by a wiry, nervous looking man in horn-rimmed glasses, picked us up at the Hotel Kreoli in the late afternoon. The cab wasn't a Mercedes, but it was still a nice mid-sized car. We left Athens and accelerated through the suburbs past the Port of Piraeus toward the city of Corinth.

The Peloponnese region where we were heading is like a colossal island, except where it is joined to the mainland at the city of Corinth. The six-kilometer-long canal, which we crossed in the taxi, severs the connection and links the Aegean Sea to the Gulf of Corinth. From then on, we flew at breakneck speed.

Much of the road ran along sheer cliffs above the sea. An approaching bus or truck would result in our driver playing a hair-raising game of chicken to see who would monopolize the middle of the road.

When we came to a village, we passed through it at a crawl, dodging pedestrians, sheep, and stray dogs. There were many small towns, one after another, along the way. At dusk, we were alarmed to notice our driver turning off his headlights when the street lights along the road were on. Al and I, with the children between us, exchanged wide-eyed terrified looks, but kept quiet.

Americans are accustomed to interstate highways, which bypass all the charm and personality of our small towns. We go flying down the freeway with our eyes fixed on the car in front of us. Greece's highway system of the 1970s was like traveling in the USA prior to 1957. The roads went right through the center of each picturesque village, making travel more interesting, but not as efficient.

We reached Patras, which was the largest city along our way. With an encouraging lilt to his voice, Al said, "We're nearly home."

In about half an hour, the cab approached our village in semi-darkness, but we could see groves of trees surrounding us along the road. Kato was a rustic village inhabited by about five hundred people with a few more on outlying farms. The small town had few paved streets, but the stucco houses were neatly kept, and the yards were tidy.

Al directed the cabbie to the town's center square, and then we drove one block on a dirt street to our flat-roofed white stucco house. It stood at the intersection of two rough unpaved roads.

By the glow of the street light, I could see it was one of the newest and nicest homes in town. We would pay forty-three American dollars a month rent, which included water and electricity. Our driver left us there, and we were eager to explore our new home.

Al, holding Matt in his arms, opened the filigree metal front door with frosted glass window panes so we could enter.

"This is it. This is our new home. We are the first family to live here."

"It's nice," I said, my eyes scanning around the entry hall. I was carrying Tammy. "We've never had a brand new house before."

Making our way from room to room, we found the spaces were generously sized with marble floors and high ceilings. Large windows were covered with blue shutters on the outside.

We made our way to the kitchen. I saw it had a sink with

running water and a small counter.

"Where are you hiding the refrigerator?" I asked hesitantly.

"We don't have one yet, but I'm working on it. It looks like it will have to come from Patras."

My mind instantly started working out how to feed my family without a fridge. The refrigerator is a central feature of American life. How did the early settlers keep their food cold?

Near the sink a three-burner hot plate, which required a match to light, was hooked up to a propane tank. There was no oven. A table, four chairs, and a small free-standing cabinet were arranged on one side of the room. There was a highchair for Tammy. A plastic five gallon water container stood near the sink.

Al saw me eyeing the water jug.

"The Americans haven't been able to drink the local water without getting sick," he said.

"Oh, wow."

"But it's okay to wash with it. It won't hurt you," he added. "I get the drinking water at the detachment. There's a big tank out there called a 'water buffalo'."

I felt a momentary apprehension about the challenges we might endure, but the gratitude I felt from having my family back together overcame it. I realized right away I would have to do some creative cooking in this kitchen. I would need to shop for fresh food daily, but that would be healthy for my family.

Down the hall was a large bedroom. It was bare, except for a metal-framed double bed with a handmade mattress. A stack of folded linens waited to be spread upon the bed. There was no closet.

"I guess we can keep our clothes in the big suitcase until I figure something out," I said.

The second bedroom was set up with a crib for Tammy and a single bed for Matt. Both had hand-sewn mattresses. I think the Greeks would have used the room for dining, rather than sleeping. They would have all slept together in the big bedroom.

"How in the world did you furnish a whole house without a vehicle to haul stuff?" I questioned.

"Well, the Greeks are very helpful and resourceful merchants. They volunteer to bring whatever you buy to your house. Some of it came by donkey."

"I appreciate you doing all this so we can be together again." I reached up and kissed him.

"The best news is we have an indoor bathroom, which is rare in Kato."

Shocked, I turned my eyes heavenward and mouthed the words, "Thank you, Lord."

The possibility of an outhouse hadn't entered my consciousness. Nothing would be taken for granted from that day forward.

Our wonderful indoor bathroom had hot water, a small bathtub with a built-in seat, and a telephone shower, meaning the shower head looked like a telephone receiver and sat in a cradle on the edge of the bathtub. It would work well for bathing the kids and shampooing our hair.

We went out the kitchen door to inspect the moonlit back yard and found a good-sized vegetable and herb garden growing there.

"The landlord's mother tends the garden and picks the produce," Al explained.

"Speaking of food, I'm starving. What smells so good?" I said.

The seductive perfume of meat cooking over charcoal attracted us like ants to a sugar bowl. The pleasant fragrance grabbed us and drew us to the town square. We found a street vendor there selling shish kabobs he called *souvlaki*. After removing the skewer of meat from the grill, the man squeezed lime juice over the bite-sized pieces of charred lamb. Then he put a small cube of toasted bread on the pointy end of the stick.

We bought a few of the kabobs and some sesame seed-covered bread from another street vendor. With our dinner wrapped in waxed paper, we headed back to settle into our new home.

We found the rustic food delicious and satisfying. It was like finding an anchor we could rely on while we were surrounded by so many uncertainties.

We got the beds made and settled in for the night. It was quiet and very dark. We slept soundly.

The next morning in the light of day, I looked around our new neighborhood. I saw plain square homes with plastered exteriors. Most were one story with flat roofs like ours. The walls were whitewashed. The doors, trim, and shutters were painted Greek flag blue or wasabi green. Red geraniums grew exuberantly in old olive oil tins.

Some colors were bright, and some were softly faded by the bleaching sunshine, but they were all pure colors. The intense blue sky amplified all the hues beneath it.

Reflecting for a quiet moment before my family awoke, I realized how profoundly different our lives would be for the next year. This would not be a neat and tidy three day excursion planned by a travel agent. We were going in deep and immersing ourselves into this culture so foreign to us.

I had left behind most of the conveniences I had come to rely on. With two children in diapers and no washer and dryer, fridge, oven, or vacuum cleaner, I would be living like a pioneer woman.

This would be an experience we would cherish, but one which would make us appreciate our American way of life even more than we had before. I was ready for the challenge of this new frontier. I thought, *This is meant to be.*

Cue the music:
"Happy Together"
The Turtles

3 – LIKE TO GET TO KNOW YOU

Greek people passing by our house would call out to us, *"Kali me'ra,"* which we learned from our American friends meant 'good morning'.

Soon we were calling, *"Kali me'ra,"* back to them. The townspeople were friendly. We learned to say, *"Kali spe'ra,"* wishing them a 'good evening'.

Hospitality abounds in Greece. Guests are always offered the best chair, the best food, and the best drink their host has to offer. A love of welcoming visitors seems to dwell in the hearts of Greek people. A foreigner couldn't find a more agreeable place to wander. We felt very fortunate for the warm acceptance we received.

Most of the neighbors we met knew only three English words: 'Nixon', 'cowboy,' and 'Texas'. Richard Nixon was president in 1971, and this was before the Watergate scandal broke and made him infamous.

The townsfolk always referred to Kato as 'Kato, Achaia', which led me to believe there might be another Kato in Greece. Achaia is the region, what we might call a state, where Kato is located. Patras is the capital of Achaia. The region covers 1,263 square miles.

Movies are international ambassadors. The Greeks we met had seen American cowboy movies dubbed in their language, and we had seen *Zorba the Greek* and *Never on Sunday.* We all had preconceived notions about each other drawn from the films we had seen.

It wasn't unusual to see Greeks break into spontaneous dancing and singing. They seemed buoyant with happiness, but I didn't see any of them throwing dinner plates like Frisbees while we were living in Greece. Perhaps I just didn't go to the right *tavernas*.

Shopping daily got us out of the house and into our new community quickly. We inherited a baby stroller which, with a little ingenuity, we converted to a two-seater. Then both the children could ride while we walked the road to the town center.

A block from our house, strategically positioned near the bus station, was a street vendor selling rolls and sweet breads from a glass case on a cart. We often made a purchase to munch on while we promenaded down to the main road.

Al would say to the vendor, *"Parakalo?"* meaning 'please?'

Each day we observed our neighbors sweeping the front steps of their homes with handmade brooms. Some of the brooms had short handles, which at first I thought were broken. Later I saw the short brooms for sale downtown along with traditional brooms.

After sweeping, they washed the doors and steps using a bucket of water. Though the homes were modest, they were kept neat and clean. The homeowners took great pride in their humble dwellings. The storekeepers swept and washed their store fronts each day as well.

We found that most of the shops specialized in selling one food item like seafood or vegetables. We learned to say, *"Po'so ka'ni?"* to ask how much an item cost. We could say, *"Ef karisto,"* with a smile to thank the merchants and store keepers. Since the Greek language has its own alphabet, it is difficult to learn. Two or three word phrases were the most we were able to master. We didn't learn to read many words, either. We saw the same Greek letters on signs outside every bakery, hotel, or restaurant and simply deduced their meanings.

A few stores had the household goods we needed to set up our home. There weren't many plastic items available though, and those they had didn't seem to be very durable. They weren't like the Tupperware back home.

I was slightly revolted when I saw the Kato meat market. Cleaned carcasses, some with heads, hung on meat hooks just inside the front windows. Modern Americans like their meat wrapped in tidy plastic-covered packages. We don't really like to ponder where our food comes from, but I got used to seeing the cadavers before long. The shop sold various creatures from rabbits to sheep, but beef was seldom found. We bonded with the butcher and communicated that we wanted *vodino* if it was ever available. Our paperback phonetic English to Greek phrase book came in handy.

After our request, the butcher dutifully notified us when he had some beef. I think we dined on a few dairy cows that died of old age during our stay in Greece, but they tasted wonderful to us. We only had beef three times during the year we were there, other than the occasions when we dined at the American NCO Clubs at Araxos or Athens.

Cue the music:
"You Ain't Goin' Nowhere"
The Byrds

When foreigners from countries with healthy diets move to America, they lose their resistance to disease quickly. Our fast food, high sugar diet makes the new arrivals susceptible to diabetes, heart disease, and cancer like the rest of us. Our family was reversing this process by immersing ourselves in the Mediterranean diet and lifestyle.

In the USA a perfect meal is a big slab of steak so large it hangs off the edge of the plate. A huge baked potato with lots of butter is the favorite side dish. We have a salad, but it's swimming in a dressing of saturated fat. These foods wouldn't be available to us in our day-to-day life in Greece.

A thick, well-marbled steak epitomizes the American dream. We consider steak to be one of our constitutional rights! Beef has shaped our country and our way of life. It made the cowboy a symbol of adventurous virility, made ranchers rich, and created railroad and meatpacking empires. Beef put Chicago and Kansas City on the map.

A weekly trip to a steakhouse is an American family ritual. Charcoal smoke billowing from grills in backyards across the country evokes a Pavlovian response. Becoming a vegetarian in America really goes against the grain.

Sadly, few of the cattle spend their lives lolling around the pasture these days. They may start out there, but they are soon sent to a feedlot for fattening. The meatpacking giants in Chicago and Kansas City figured this method out way back in the days when cattle were driven to market on the hoof. The bovines arrived rather worse for wear and a little too skinny. Fattening before slaughter became part of the operation.

Today the cattle in feedlots are fed mostly corn and other grains. I've even heard of them being fed stale candy, wrappers and all. So much for the grass fed cycle of life.

All the foods we enjoyed in Greece were either at the peak of freshness or perfectly aged. The Greeks seemed to have an innate sense about food preservation which provided a taste explosion for us.

Only one store in Kato sold a variety of grocery staples. It reminded me of a general store from the American pioneer era or an ancient apothecary shop from a Dickens novel. The store looked as if it had been there for two or three hundred years. The wood display shelves were dark with age. Canned goods with red, blue, and yellow labels looked like pop art to me. Glass jars encased mysterious contents.

The smell of fragrant items mingled with the more odiferous, giving the place its own signature earthy scent. The store had one small refrigerated case, but cow's milk and butter were not found in it. I continued to buy powdered and canned milk in Athens at the commissary for our family's needs.

Yellow cheddar cheeses were not found in Kato. Creamy white Feta cheese made from sheep's milk was sold in the store and at the outdoor markets on Saturday. It was good crumbled over our *salata* or a pasta dish.

No shopping carts or baskets were available. The shopper would choose their items and place them on the counter to be added up by the storekeepers.

Fresh eggs, laid that morning, were nestled in tissue paper on a table. The eggs were sold individually, not by the dozen. A massive stoneware crock held unpitted Kalamata olives. I dipped the amount I wanted into a waxed paper cup using a large slotted spoon.

Beautifully decorated metal tins were stacked in attractive displays. Each one held about half a gallon of olive oil. Most Americans wouldn't dream of buying olive oil in that quantity, unless they owned a restaurant. The price would be prohibitive. But in Greece in the 1970s, olive oil was the only oil used for cooking, and its abundance kept the cost down.

Greece produces the most olives and olive oil of all the Mediterranean countries. The most widely cultivated variety for oil is the Koroneiki. The olives are small, but bear heavily. The fruit is high in polyphenols, the natural substance in plants found to reduce the risk of heart disease and cancer.

Three-fourths of Greek olive oil is the very best, extra virgin. I still remember the taste of the delicious oil on my tongue. Its color was a light chartreuse green. The extra virgin oil was from the first pressing of the olives. It had a fresh, full-of-life flavor I've never found in any olive oil I've tried since then.

Dry pasta shells, beans, macaroni, egg noodles, and tomato paste were staples I relied on to feed my family. The tomato paste was sliced off a brick-sized log as solid as any cheese log I had served on Christmas back in the States. I showed the woman who ran the store how much tomato paste I wanted by making a cutting motion with my finger. She sliced off the paste and wrapped it in waxed paper for me.

I purchased flour, which must have come from the mainland. The Plains of Thessaly supported cattle and grain production, which the Peloponnese did not.

I accumulated my small group of items on the counter and the woman looked them over, mentally tallying them up.

"Po'so ka'ni, parakalo?" I asked. The woman wrote the number 38 on a piece of paper and said, *"Trianta okto."* I smiled and handed her the correct number of drachmas. It was a little over one American dollar, and I could make several meals from these ingredients.

"Ef karisto," she said, smiling at me. Our neighbors seemed to appreciate us trying to communicate in their language. I learned, or I might say I absorbed, the numbers one through ten from my daily shopping excursions.

1 - *ena*
2 - *dio*
3 - *tria*
4 - *tessera*
5 - *penda*
6 - *exi*
7 - *epta*
8 - *okto*
9 - *enea*
10 - *deke*

You may see commonality with the numbers of the Romance languages of Spanish, French, and Italian. Many English words have Greek roots.

The storekeepers lived in the back of the shop with their children. They treated Americans like honored guests when we visited their store. The friendly folks even invited us to their son's first birthday party. The family invited all their neighbors to come and celebrated with cake and gifts, just like Americans do. The cake was a walnut cake without icing called *karythopita*.

Greek children and their families celebrate the day of their birth until they are twelve years old. After that, they celebrate on the day of the saint they are named after. The most popular saint names have huge numbers of people celebrating together on that day. What a party!

Cue the music:
"Picture Book"
The Kinks

Each time I came to buy groceries, the shopkeepers offered me an Ouzo shot and wouldn't take no for an answer. Ouzo is a licorice-flavored spirit. It is as popular in Greece as tequila is in Texas. Although I wasn't used to strong alcoholic drinks, I would drink one shot in order not to offend my new friends, say, *"Adi'o,"* and go shuffling back home lightheaded.

We adjusted to the Greek custom of closing the shops from noon until two, three, or as late as four o'clock in the afternoon for the shopkeeper's lunch and rest time. Sturdy corrugated metal doors were closed over the front of the shops, and they were buttoned up tight. I have wondered if Greece is still on this relaxed time table now in the twenty-first century when the world is so frantically rushing by.

With minor changes, our neighbors in Kato were living just as their ancestors had for hundreds of years. It was as if time had stood still there in that secluded village.

In the evening, the busiest time of the day, the stores were all open. The streets filled with shoppers, and people congregated around the square to socialize. The Greek families usually dined on their evening meal around nine or ten o'clock. *Tavernas* served dinner as late as 1:00 am.

The townspeople were extremely neighborly and affectionate to us, even though we stood out as foreigners in their village. As we walked by, they would rush out of their houses to shake our hands and say, *"Yah soo,"* which meant 'hello' and *"Ti kanis?"* meaning 'how are you?' Our short reply was, *"Polee kala",* 'very fine'.

They found the kids' pale blond hair to be fascinating, but they hated the fact that Matt sucked his thumb. They would pull his thumb from his mouth and say, *"Ochi, ochi,"* meaning 'no, no'. They didn't know he had exited the womb sucking his thumb. It proved to be a hard habit to break.

Strangely, it didn't seem to bother them when six-year-old Greek children sucked pacifiers or sat on their mother's lap to be spoon fed. The children looked robust, but for some unknown reason they had to be coaxed to eat. I chalked it up to cultural differences.

Cultural differences sometimes cause visitors to foreign lands to inadvertently insult native country folks. For instance, the University of Texas Longhorns 'hook 'em horns' hand sign is seen as a brazenly satanic symbol throughout most of the world. When in Asia, don't wear your shoes into the house.

In France, your dinner companions will expect to see both of your hands above the table. That custom would cause charm school instructors in the deep American South to curl up and die with embarrassment. Below the Mason-Dixon Line, a debutante must keep her left hand firmly anchored in her lap at the dining table.

Greece seems to have more negative hand signs than almost any other country, except Italy. Even worse, the bad signs in

Greece mean good things most everywhere else, which can cause chaotic confusion.

For instance, holding up all five fingers, which in America means 'hi' or that you're swearing to tell the truth, means 'go to hell' in Greece. Likewise, the 'v for victory' or 'peace sign', when turned around with palm inward, means 'up yours' in Greece.

The affirming 'thumbs-up' hitchhiking sign means 'get stuffed' to Greeks. Good luck to any uninformed American hitcher trying to thumb a ride in Greece. You can see how easily mistakes like these can be made by inexperienced travelers.

We found nodding up and down meant 'no' to Greeks and left to right meant 'yes', just the opposite from what these gestures mean in the USA. "Nay", a negative response in English, means 'yes' in Greek.

We were flabbergasted to see men walking down the street hand in hand or with their arms around each other. Later, we learned this was a sign of respect. We quickly grasped which words we should never use, unless we were ready for fisticuffs. We were feeling farther and farther away from middle America.

From our wire-fenced backyard, we could see into the yards of our neighbors. Plants and herbs potted in metal buckets and old tins decorated the outdoor areas. Most families had vegetable gardens growing. Bunches of herbs were tied up in twine, drying under the eaves of their houses.

Some of the neighbors had outdoor tables for dining. They didn't have patio furniture that you would see in America. Their traditional straight-backed wood kitchen chairs and tables were brought outside. The Greek families enjoyed meals in the open air quite often. Their repasts were spread on immaculate white starched tablecloths.

Some of the nearby residents had large looms set up in shaded areas outside their houses. They made rugs, shawls, and bags. Embroidery and various types of needlework were done by most of the village girls and their mothers. The handiwork was a pastime, as well as a way to adorn their simple dwellings. The contrast between spare whitewashed rooms and the fine embellished handiwork was striking and elegant.

The housewives of Kato were trim with strong shoulders, and they usually wore dresses and aprons. Daily, the local women worked outside, washing clothes and hanging them on the clothes line while listening to the Greek version of soap operas on the radio. I couldn't understand the dialogue, but the dramatic organ music was universal.

Soon I was also out in my backyard leaning over a tub, scrubbing our clothes on a corrugated wash board. I moved Tammy's high chair outside, and the backyard became an extension of the house. Matt played among the garden rows. Al rigged up a clothes line between two branches. Our garments and dozens of diapers could be seen flapping in the breeze.

I never owned an iron or ironing board during our time in Greece, so I had a yearlong reprieve from that dreaded household chore. The airmen's uniforms got laundered and pressed at the detachment.

Early in the morning, the neighborhood wives shook out brilliantly colored Flokati rugs and hung them over their porch railings to air. The thick, shaggy rugs were handmade from the wool of local sheep. Flokati rugs have been used by discerning decorators and interior designers for over one hundred years. Pick up the latest glossy interior design magazine and compare it to an edition from the 1930s. Both are likely to have a picture of a Flokati on a floor or draped over a piece of furniture to add luxurious texture to the room's décor.

The wool is spun into yarn and woven to create large loops, which are then cut by hand. Each authentic Flokati is carried to a mountain waterfall, where it is washed for hours. The power of the waterfall fluffs the yarn into an incomparable soft downy pile. The Flokati can then be dyed a bright color or left the natural soft white. Flokati rugs are still made as they have been for hundreds of years. Factories have never been able to duplicate the quality produced by the ancient method.

The village boys played up and down the dirt streets by our house with their ever-present soccer ball. I rarely saw them play with any other toy. All the Kato lads could head the ball and maneuver it down the street like a pro. The boys wore shorts, t-shirts, and t-strap leather shoes. Groups of four or five would play a game similar to hacky sack with the soccer ball, never letting it touch the ground. The girls, usually wearing dresses or skirts, avoided the rough play. They seemed to stay indoors more than the boys, probably helping their mothers with household chores.

Only a few of the most fortunate youths attended school. Those who did often visited us to try out a few English words they had learned. The local youngsters seemed to delight in our children, patting them tenderly on the backs of their tiny hands and touching their flaxen blond hair. Matt and Tammy would stay inside the gated porch on the front of our house, waiting for the Kato children to come by to visit them. The porch, with its wrought iron railing and gate, served us as an oversized play pen. The floor was laid with square marble tiles. The kids pretended the enclosure was their own little house.

Grandmotherly Greek women dressed in black from head to toe frequently walked down the roads by our house. We learned they were the venerable matriarchs of the multi-generational families living around us. Our landlord's mother was one of them. She was a well-upholstered and cheerful lady who looked as if she were wearing every piece of clothing she owned at once. She even had strips of wool wrapped around her legs.

The village grandmothers' heavy black costumes never

varied, no matter how hot the weather became. I made the assumption these ladies were widows. The only exposed skin they showed was their face from eyes to chin and their hands. These parts told the story of many years of hard work outdoors in fields and olive groves. They showed decades of fetching water, gathering firewood, cooking for their families, milking, and sewing. The work of these fine women contributed much to the Greek way of life.

Lacking ovens in their own homes, the matriarchs carried large pans of chicken or rabbit surrounded with vegetables to the bakery to be cooked for a small fee. On special occasions, it was lamb and potatoes. Before the evening meal, they would return to retrieve their family's baked dinner. We would see the little band marching home to their family tables, full of good spirits and chattering all the way. The fragrant meals they carried perked up our appetites. The townspeople of Kato did a lot of walking. It was purposeful though, not for exercise.

Scientists have learned that walking on rocky or uneven cobblestone streets gives elderly people resistance to falling and sharpens their sense of balance. When an acrobat stands on a teeter board, they train their body and brain to react instantly. Walking over the rough terrain in the streets of Kato did the same thing.

Donkeys were used by villagers as beasts of burden. They were fitted with wooden pack saddles cinched tightly. The small creatures carried huge loads of firewood, baskets of vegetables and fruit, household goods, and sometimes riders. I felt sympathy for the tiny animals bearing such heavy weights. The little burros served as the pickup trucks of Kato.

Donkeys navigated Greece's rough terrain for centuries before paved roads existed. A vacant lot across the street from our house was often used as a donkey parking lot on Saturday market days.

A frequent and welcome visitor to the neighborhood was the trash man, even though we had little trash, since we used almost no processed foods. We recycled most jars and containers out of necessity. The trash man stood on the footboard of his horse-drawn wagon holding the leather reins. He wore a billed cap made from heavy wool, which had the ear flaps tied up. I never saw him sit down on the wagon's wood seat. He was tall, and he towered over me as I lifted my small pail up to him. He emptied the bucket into the back of the wagon. For this valuable service, we paid him a few drachmas.

Cue the music:
"Lookin' Out My Back Door"
Creedence Clearwater Revival

4 – WE MAY NEVER PASS THIS WAY (AGAIN)

The older men of our village gathered daily at the pastry shop to talk. They discussed politics, smoked, and sipped espresso coffee. Ottoman occupiers had introduced coffee and cafés called *kafeneions* to the Greeks. They embraced the wonderful beans and made coffee an integral part of their lives.

The modern patriarchs of Kato wore tailored wool sport coats and pleated wool trousers, and they usually sat at outdoor tables. Their shirts were buttoned all the way up to their necks. Most of the men were clean shaven.

Worry beads clicked in many hands. The beads were popular as stress relievers, to occupy the hands, to avoid smoking, or just to pass the time. The smoking angle didn't seem to be working though, since the hand not moving the beads usually held a strong-smelling unfiltered cigarette. The smoke permeated the bakery items, ruining them for me. My husband's favorite dessert is Boston cream pie. The Greek bakery sold a miniature version of the treat he couldn't resist, even though they smelled strongly of secondhand smoke.

The American airmen started wearing Henley-style striped Greek men's pajama tops as casual shirts, which seemed to agitate the well-dressed gentlemen considerably. When they spotted a pajama-clad American on the street, the dapper Greek fellows began looking askance, gesturing, and talking loudly.

"These shirts are so comfortable. They make a nice change from fatigues," Al said, looking at his reflection in our little bathroom mirror, the only one in the house.

"I don't think the Greek men at the café like seeing you in them. They seem upset."

"I don't think they like 'hot pants' either, but what do they know about American fashions?"

During the hot season of the year, the American wives wore shorts, just as we would have back home. This was when the short shorts called 'hot pants' first came into style. Our immodest apparel brought stares from all the natives of Kato, since such garments were never worn by adult Greeks. They seemed to find our clothes peculiar and a little risqué.

About nine months into our year in Greece, I took a risk and went to a local hair salon. I had been trimming my own bangs regularly, but I wanted a professional trim, shampoo, and styling. Even with my trusty phrase book, I was never able to communicate what I wanted to the hairdressers. I pantomimed a haircut using my fingers as pretend scissors. All they did was style my hair. They acted afraid to cut it. I guess I was the first foreigner who had wandered into their beauty shop.

The bus station was on the town square a block from our house and was usually a beehive of activity. Few of the townspeople of Kato owned cars. In order to travel to Patras to shop, visit the winery, or go to the hospital, they traveled by buses, which ran hourly. It was common to see travelers carrying goats, chickens, and large wicker-covered demijohn bottles on the bus. The enormous bottles appeared to hold about five gallons of wine from the Winery Achaia Clauss, which was located in the countryside near Patras. They were as large as water cooler bottles seen in American office buildings. The jugs were rigged with leather straps or ropes to make carrying them easier.

Our landlord was a rosy-cheeked cherub of a man in his forties who always wore a dark wool sports jacket. He seemed very happy with a big smile on his face most of the time. He and his family managed the bus station.

We were astounded when we visited their tiny apartment at

the side of the station. We found their family of five, which included the grandmother, living in a space smaller than our kitchen. They all slept in one room with very little space to walk around the bed.

I felt bad that our family was taking their luxurious large home while they lived like gherkins in a jar. The landlord reassured me through our translator, the local cabbie, that he had built the house we occupied as an investment. Year after year, American families would live there. Their rent would pay for the house. When he owned the house free and clear, he and his family would move in. They would luxuriate in the spacious residence and make it their permanent home.

He was a genuinely clever businessman, willing to wait patiently for his reward. I hope his hard work paid off, and he finally achieved his dream for his family.

Gasoline was the one item that was expensive in Greece. A liter, which is slightly more than our quart, sold for the equivalent of thirty-six cents American money, which means a gallon was about $1.30. By contrast, gas was selling for thirty-six cents a gallon back in the States in 1971.

The Greek answer to high gas prices was the three-wheeled vehicle known in Kato as a *Zundapp*. The *Zundapp* was the clever result of splicing a German *Zundapp* motorbike with a truck chassis. The first transformations of motorbikes into three-wheeled trucks happened during World War II while Greece was occupied by Nazi forces. After the war, motorcycles and military vehicles were abandoned along roadsides all across Greece. Adroit shade tree mechanics created their *Zundapp* three-wheelers with remarkably useful results.

By the late Fifties, Greek factories were producing the vehicles, as well as the needed replacement parts. Some of the *Zundapps* we saw around Kato had enclosed cabs for the driver, but most did not. The fuel efficient three-wheelers were the most frequently seen vehicle in Kato, vastly outnumbering cars or large trucks. I always wanted to ride a *Zundapp*, but sadly, I never got the chance.

Near the bus station was the kiosk, the Greek equivalent of a convenience store. The wood structure, slightly larger than a phone booth, offered newspapers and magazines, cigarettes and matches, postcards, stamps, maps, and our primary interests, candy, cookies, and ice cream bars. We called them ice cream, but I think the bars were ice milk, probably made with sheep's milk.

The outside of the kiosk was plastered with goods offered for sale. From the moment I tasted the extremely dark chocolate *sokolata* bar, I was in love. At only five drachmas, the equivalent of seventeen cents, they were a steal. The distinctive wrapper was a beautiful shade of blue. I can still remember the delectable flavor, sweet but with a slight edge of bitterness. Al and the kids loved the Papadopoulos Biscuits, which were cream-filled sandwich cookies sold in a sleeve of eight. These treats sweetened our time in Kato.

The Greek Orthodox Church was the only church in Kato. Ninety eight percent of the Greek people in the 1970s professed to be Greek Orthodox. The daily lives of the citizens were deeply entwined with the church and the priests. The strong families we saw in Kato seemed to have the church as their foundation.

Curious, we peered through the open doors of the chapel to see the holy figures painted on the wall above the brass-encrusted altar. Elaborate standing brass candelabras holding tall beeswax tapers stood nearby. The sweet fragrance of the candles mingled with the scent of mint and basil.

We saw the priests all around town, garbed in rippling black full-length robes and tall black hats. They wore abundant chin whiskers and walked almost everywhere they went. The clergymen were greatly revered in the community, and it was customary for church members to kiss the priest's hand upon meeting him.

The beliefs of the Greek Orthodox Church are the same as most Christian churches. The Holy Trinity, Jesus as Lord and Savior, and the resurrection of Jesus are the fundamental doctrines. The priests are allowed to marry. The Orthodox services are carried out in the original Greek used to write the New Testament. The church can trace its long history from the twelve original Apostles to the present day.

The Greek Orthodox Church differs in their use of the old Julian calendar to calculate the date for Easter. Greeks usually celebrate Easter on a Sunday other than the one believers in the US observe. Easter is the biggest holiday of the year for Greeks, of much more solemn importance than Christmas. Easter is the time when many big city dwellers return to their home villages to spend time with their families.

It would be hard to imagine the United States with only one church. America's foundation of religious freedom has fostered our diverse multitude of denominations, although most share the same basic beliefs.

We saw a few wedding couples emerge from the church during our year in Kato. Both the bride and groom wore crowns of white flowers. The brides' gowns were modest white satin, but they were lovely in their simplicity. Most young people lived at home with their family until they were married.

The bride was expected to make a collection, or trousseau, of embellished linens and handiwork to adorn the couple's new home. These projects probably took her years to create. The items were brought to the new residence with great ceremony by donkey.

More funerals took place in Kato than weddings. Orthodox beliefs of the time affirmed that the body be buried within twenty-four hours of death. Embalming and cremation were unacceptable, because the decomposition process was believed to be part of the forgiveness of sins.

The casket was visible through the glass walls of the horse-drawn hearse as it traveled slowly and reverently to the cemetery on the outskirts of town. The driver wore a black top hat, and the two horse team wore feather plumes on their heads. The adornments looked a little tattered from many wearings. The mourners, wearing their best clothes, walked down the street behind the hearse. These final minutes above ground were some of the grandest moments of these spare and Spartan lives.

Three to seven years after a burial, the remains were exhumed and moved to the family tomb or an ossuary. The degree of decomposition and whiteness of the bones signified that forgiveness had been attained.

Cue the music:
"Turn! Turn! Turn!"
The Byrds

Araxos Air Force Detachment was a small outpost. Only about ninety American airmen were stationed there, working in coordination with the Hellenic Air Force. Of those, less than ten had wives and families living in Kato. With such small numbers, we had to form a community and help each other. We shared household goods, food, and exchanged babysitting. Anyone traveling to Athens always offered to bring back needed items for the other families.

For the first month of our life in Greece, Al was picked up for the twelve mile ride to work at the detachment by other airmen who had vehicles. While visiting Athens, he applied for his international driver's license. In due time he received it, and we inherited a car from one of the departing Americans. We paid nothing for it.

The car was a 1959 Renault with faded red paint the color of a Spanish peanut. That, combined with its squat, rounded shape, inspired us to nickname it 'the Peanut'. The engine was in the rear, and it had a crank you could use for emergency starting, just like an old Model T. The crank came in handy several times when the battery began to fail us toward the end of the summer. By the end of our year in Greece, we had to push start it. I would sit in the driver's seat and steer with the clutch pedal down. Al and whoever else might be there would push the car. When it got up some speed, I would pop out the clutch and the Peanut would usually start. Even though the twelve–year–old Peanut looked worn out, it ran real well once we got it started. We were excited to have our own car. Nothing makes you appreciate something like going without.

The Peanut only held four gallons of fuel, but got fantastic gas mileage. We got to know the local mechanic and his crew of young apprentices who were able to fix any problems that arose in exchange for a carton of American cigarettes. The mechanic would say, *"Avrio,"* meaning 'tomorrow'. He meant 'come back tomorrow, and your car will be fixed.'

From the mechanic, we also learned the words *endoxi,* meaning 'okay', and *etsi ketsi,* meaning 'so so'. These words were what Americans would call slang, but they became very useful to us. The mechanic and Al could only exchange a few words due to the language barrier, but they became fast friends.

The grease monkey usually had a handkerchief knotted at each corner on his head like a hat. We saw field and construction workers all over the country of Greece wearing handkerchiefs like that.

We pulled out the covers from the Peanut's door panels, so every inch of the interior space could be utilized when we made a supply run to Athens. The Air Force Commissary there had American products, and best of all they had disposable diapers, which were relatively new on the market. With two children in diapers, the Pampers were my most coveted item. When we couldn't get Pampers, I had to make cotton flannel diapers and wash them by hand in the tub in the backyard.

The dentists and doctors used by the Araxos airmen were also at the American airbase in Athens. "Al, isn't your lower second molar bothering you about now?" I would ask. "We could use some Pampers."

"Oh, I get it. I'll see if I can get an appointment," Al would reply with a wink.

Upon our return to Kato, we traveled to each American home to unload their requested commissary items. They anticipated our arrival as much as they looked forward to Christmas. It was interesting to see what each household considered an absolute necessity.

One of our first rides in the Peanut was to the Araxos Air Force Detachment where Al worked. The curvy, narrow roadway followed the coastline. We saw vegetable gardens tucked in here and there along the way. The planters had devised an ingenious way of tenting the rows with plastic sheeting over arched supports, thereby extending the growing season by creating a makeshift greenhouse.

Beekeepers had hives scattered over the hilly fields. The bees gathered nectar from the orange blossoms, almond trees, and wildflowers and herbs growing over the craggy knolls. An established hive can produce up to sixty pounds of honey a year. There is a lot to know before you reap that kind of liquid gold, though. I'm sure the valuable apian knowledge was taught by one generation to the next.

Honey was the only sweetener we saw in Kato. Beekeepers sold their pleasing products at the Saturday market on the square. Some of the jars contained chunks of honeycomb, which were both beautiful and interesting to look at. The combs are six-sided wax hexagons created by the bees. Hexagon is a word with Greek roots. *Hex* means 'six', and *gonia* means 'corner'.

The cells are the perfect structure. Hexagons take less wax than any other shape would require and are stronger. The honeybees fill the cells with honey and seal the ends with wax. The beekeeper sedates the bees and drives them from the hive with puffs of smoke. He then harvests the honeycomb. The sealed ends are sliced off, and the honey is extracted.

The empty comb is returned to the hive to form a foundation for new combs to be built. That requires less work for the bees, so they use less energy and consume less honey, leaving more to be harvested next time. Because of its purity, honey is the only food that never spoils.

If you didn't drive too fast, you might spy blue metal or wooden boxes on tall spindly legs tucked in along the roadway. They were usually found near a sharp curve in the road that might be considered dangerous. These sacred places were roadside shrines to saints.

The shrines around Kato weren't fancy. They were plain with a pitched roof that had a cross on top and a windowed door on the front. They usually contained a picture of the saint, a candle, and a bunch of flowers or a sprig of basil or mint. In neighborhoods wealthier than Kato, the shrines were more elaborate. Some were detailed replicas of the local churches.

Occasionally, we could hear bells faintly ringing in the distance as we drove along the lane. The sound got louder as we approached. Then we saw animals moving across the highway.

We often had to stop the car for herds of sheep and goats being driven across our path, but the delays didn't annoy us. We adored seeing the flocks, which would totally engulf our car. Smiles broke out on our faces every time. The soft bleating sound they made was music to our ears. The nuzzling sheep were affectionate and seemed to enjoy seeing us, too. In 1971 in

Greece, a person could still aspire to be a shepherd.

Sheep and goat herding is one of the world's oldest occupations. A fable says the god who created Greece sifted all the soil and used just the rocks to form the country. The rough and rugged terrain in Greece, which isn't useful for planting crops, is perfect for raising sheep and goats. Sheep and goats can get all the nutrients they need from grazing, except when nursing their young. A milking ewe or doe will need some supplemental protein.

Sheep are high yield commodities, giving wool, milk, and meat. An experienced shearer will trim the coat close each spring, removing the fleece all in one piece. Sheep and goat's milk is naturally homogenized. The creamy particles don't separate from the milk the way cow's milk does. That makes it easy to digest. The milk is well tolerated by people who are allergic to cow's milk, and it makes delectable cheese. Luxurious soaps and lotions can also be made from the milk. Sheep and goats are a good match with the Greek bent for frugality. Nothing is wasted.

There are two drawbacks to sheep rearing. First, they can't be left unattended or they will scatter, and second, they need to be moved from pasture to pasture frequently to avoid overgrazing. Grasses take about twenty days to grow back to a height where they can be grazed again. The constantly wary shepherd must keep the flock together and safe from predators, attend lambing, and deliver the stock to the shearer in the spring.

The shepherd must be vigilant, watching for cast sheep. Sheep, especially pregnant ewes, sometimes tip over onto their backs and cannot right themselves. They can become agitated and panic stricken. If not helped to their feet quickly, the cast sheep may die.

Gentle-natured sheep have been wrongly branded as stupid

animals because of their flocking and following instincts. These instincts are actually their only defense against predators. Scientists have found that sheep demonstrate the ability to learn and remember things as well as monkeys do. They made these discoveries while using sheep for researching human brain disorders.

Sick sheep have also exhibited the innate ability to seek out plants to eat that will heal their illnesses. They seem to recognize poisonous plants and avoid them. Of course, goats can eat almost anything, including poison ivy and poison oak without being harmed.

We found herds of sheep and goats crossing roads everywhere we traveled in Greece, except for the bustling streets of Athens. There were herds in the high meadows above Athens, though.

Along the way to the detachment, we visited a rustic fishing village on the water. People there seemed to be living even more simply than in Kato. The homes were modest. Fishermen were mending handmade nets, and some were flailing squid against a rock to tenderize them. Can you imagine the patience required to take a ball of twine and turn it into a large net strong enough to catch fish? The fathers handed down their skills to the sons. There was no local sporting goods store where the fishermen could buy such a net.

Small wooden row boats were pulled up on the sandy shore. We never saw any large fishing boats like those we had seen back home in the Gulf of Mexico. A young boy unloaded a bucket with a clear glass bottom from one of the skiffs. I believe the fishermen used the bucket to look down into the water for fish and squid. It worked like a swim mask, but they didn't get wet.

We also stopped at the American Air Force Detachment's private beach. It was covered by egg-shaped white rocks, rather than sand. The water was aqua, crystal clear, and I quickly discovered, icy cold. I shivered and looked forward to going there in warmer weather.

When we arrived at the detachment, I saw that there were only a few small buildings surrounded by a tall chain link fence. One building was the corrugated tin-roofed radio shack where Al spent his eight-hour shifts.

In the beginning, he worked three swing shifts 3:00 p.m. to 11:00 p.m., three mid shifts 11:00 p.m. to 7:00, and then he had three days off. But after two months, his schedule was changed to working nine days straight with two days off. Then in January, his shifts were changed to twelve hours. His work schedule limited our ability to venture very far from Kato.

Near the radio shack was a supply building, a barracks, and a central mess hall/Non Commissioned Officers Club. The NCO Club was the Americans' home away from home. There we could hang out and dine on beef steaks, hot dogs, chili, and grilled cheese sandwiches while listening to American music on the jukebox. Free movies were shown each night. Foosball and ping pong tables were available. Al became the detachment's ping pong champion.

The outpost had a small library containing mostly paperback books. Outside was a patio with umbrella-covered tables and chairs. The close quarters gave the 'det', as we called the detachment, a congenial atmosphere. It was like being in an old friend's den or rec room back in the States. We got to know everyone well, and felt we could depend on each other for anything, just like a family.

Occasionally, we could pick up a copy of the *Stars & Stripes* newspaper at the det to keep up with current events, but we were pretty isolated from the news happening around the world. Unless it was something earth shaking, we probably didn't hear about it until weeks later.

Once each month the paymaster would arrive from Athens

with the airmen's paychecks and American money to cash their checks. It was a day they didn't want to miss work. If an airman didn't show up to collect his pay, he would have to wait an entire month to see the paymaster again.

Outside the detachment's chain link fence, a ragged looking older woman sat on a burlap sack spread out on the dirt. Her gray hair was chopped off short, and chunks were missing. She was barefoot, and her legs bore the marks of many injuries. She wore a tattered floral print dress.

The airmen called her 'Screaming Mimi'. She would smile widely, showing her broken teeth, scream an unintelligible phrase, and reach her hand through the fence, begging for drachmas when an American passed by.

She appeared outside the det fence daily. The airmen always gave her money and food, and she would blow a kiss to thank them. One of the Greek airmen told us she had been a teacher before she was tortured by the Nazis during World War II.

Not long after we arrive in Kato, the country celebrated *Ochi* Day on October 28. The national holiday, celebrated each year since 1942, commemorates the day the Greek Prime Minister Metaxas answered Benito Mussolini's Fascist ultimatum with a fearless 'no' on that day in 1940.

Mussolini demanded Greece allow the Axis forces of Nazi Germany, Italy, and Bulgaria to enter its borders and occupy 'strategic locations' or face war. Local fables say Metaxas answered with a single word, "No!"

According to history books, what he actually said was, "Then it is war!"

Italian troops broke through the Greek border with Albania. The populace of Greece poured into the streets all over the country shouting, *"Ochi! Ochi!"* with their fists raised in anger. This gives you an insight into the patriotism and the fierce need for independence that indwells the Greek people. On October

28, 1942, when the first *Ochi* Day was defiantly observed, Greece was living under Nazi occupation.

The period of 1941-1944 was a perilously dark time for the Greek people. Resistance sprang up against the invading Axis forces. Nazi soldiers raised their Swastika flag over the Acropolis in Athens, and it loomed menacingly over the entire country. Two college students secretly climbed the face of the Acropolis and ripped down the flag in one of the first acts of resistance.

Food confiscation by the invaders caused famine and death. The resistance movement grew steadily until early summer of 1943, when many more German troops advanced into Greece, fearing an Allied Forces landing.

The Nazis began ruthless counter operations against the Greek resistance fighters. Guerillas who were caught and executed immediately were considered the fortunate ones, since execution prevented torture. Hundreds of villages were burned, and nearly a million Greeks were left homeless.

Greece in 1971 was such a peaceful place, it was hard to imagine this tragic period. Seeing this unfortunate soul waiting at the det fence was a constant reminder of the selfless multitudes who laid down their lives to keep us free. Some gave all. Could I do the same if I were in their place?

Cue the music:
"Find the Cost of Freedom"
Crosby, Stills, Nash, and Young

5 – Those Were the Days My Friend

Our lovely villa on the dirt road was built especially to stay cool during the hot, dry season of the year. The filigree metal front door could be closed and the inside glass door left open to allow a breeze to come through the house.

Now it was November, and the weather became cooler and wetter. It began to rain about one day out of every three. When it rained, the weather was similar to Seattle in winter. All we had ever heard about was 'sunny Greece', so we weren't expecting this rain and this gray gloom.

Walking on the marble floors of our house was like skating on a frozen pond. I couldn't allow the children to play on the floor. It was just too cold. They had to stay up on the bed. Tammy was missing out on crawling.

Where had the sun gone?

"Al, it's getting very chilly in here. We've got to get some kind of heater," I said. "I'm afraid the kids will get sick."

"I'll go downtown and see my friend at the appliance store. Surely he has an electric heater we could buy."

In a little while, Al returned with a kerosene heater, an electric heater, and some heavy comforters. In fact, the comforters were so heavy, turning over in bed was almost impossible. I had to keep one eye on the heaters at all times to make sure Matt didn't touch them.

"Al, we need a Flokati like our neighbors have," I said. "They are one hundred percent wool . . . warm, fluffy wool."

"Okay. We can buy one on our next trip to Athens," Al agreed.

I had brought jackets for the kids and for myself in our one carefully packed suitcase, but I had not foreseen needing to wear them inside the house.

The cool, wet winters and hot, dry summers are features of the Mediterranean climate found in only a few places on the globe. Those conditions contribute to the extraordinary success growing grapes for their nectar of the gods, olives for their liquid gold, and sheep for their wool, milk, and succulent morsels. When we arrived in Kato in early October, the grape harvest was under way.

Next, the olive harvest commenced through the end of November. A long, hot summer produces the green fruit. The best oil comes from the olives just beginning to ripen. The olives were harvested by hand.

Olive trees can live for centuries. There are a few growing in the Mediterranean region that have lived over two thousand years, and they are still bearing fruit. Besides being hearty and drought resistant, olive trees are even fire resistant.

During these fall months, large wooden, hand-cranked presses mounted on two high wagon wheels were pulled from house to house in Kato. One was for crushing grapes, and another was for pressing olives. I believe my neighbors were refilling their own wine barrels and olive oil crocks to provide for their family until the next year's harvest. Olives and their oil are considered sacred in Greece. Children are anointed with olive oil at their christening.

Extra virgin cold-pressed olive oil is a superb skin moisturizer, surpassing the most expensive beauty creams and ointments for purity and effectiveness. One would think the oil would sit on the surface of the skin, but it sinks into the pores almost instantly. The ancient Olympians, known for their exquisite bodies, slathered themselves with the prized oil.

Wine making is a more complex task than pressing olives for their oil. There is chemistry involved. The first step was crushing the unwashed grapes and stems in the community press. Then our neighbors used recipes handed down from their ancestors for the precise measure of sugar, which was added to feed the yeast and produce a delightful tasting potion.

Even the pulp of peels, seeds, and stems left in the bottom of the press wasn't thrown out. This residue is called the 'must'. It was fermented and distilled to produce *tsipouro,* a heady spirit using secret family recipes. The clear liquor warms many a Greek on cold winter nights.

Following all this, the must was used as fertilizer in the garden, orchard, or field. Nothing was wasted.

The villagers also made their own soft cheeses from their fresh goat's or sheep's milk. We saw the cheeses hanging like giant pearls from the eaves of their houses. The watery whey was being carefully drained using a cheesecloth sling. After about a day, the soft feta cheese was ready to be eaten.

We didn't find hard, aged cheeses, which are popular elsewhere in Europe, available in Kato. Aged cheeses are usually swabbed with a salt solution during their processing to inhibit mold. The solution forms a rind. That is why aged cheeses taste so salty. Rapidly made (and eaten) fresh feta cheese doesn't need the salt solution for preservation, which makes it a much healthier cheese.

A legend says that cheese was invented, or should I say discovered, by a Middle Eastern sojourner carrying some milk with him, using a lamb's stomach for a container. When he paused to take a drink, he noticed the milk had formed into firm chunks. Showing his courage, he tasted one of the chunks and found it pleasing. The rennet enzyme in the stomach had separated the milk into curds and whey, which is the first step in making most cheeses.

Being young Americans, Al and I had eaten cheddar and American cheese primarily. I had never contemplated where it came from prior to showing up in my local supermarket. I wouldn't have thought I could make my own cheese.

Dining on fresh feta cheese gave us a novel flavor to relish and opened our palates to new possibilities. It tasted as fresh as a spring day. Seeing the sheep and goats being milked in nearby backyards put us directly in touch with the source of our food, and it opened our eyes.

Most Kato residents had a few hens scratching around their yards. They provided eggs and meat. I'm sure the feathers weren't wasted, either. Some of our neighbors raised rabbits for food. The Greeks of 1971 were extremely self-sufficient and frugal people.

The daily food shopping and back yard clothes washing continued rain or shine. It was more difficult to get the clothes dried, though. Some days we had drying diapers draped all over the house.

"It's a jungle of wet diapers in here!" Al said as he dodged getting slapped in the face by one of them.

"I'm sorry about that, but I'm doing the best I can. We're still using about eighteen diapers a day. I'm having a hard time keeping up. If I don't get these dried, my only other option is to go buy more cotton flannel and make more diapers," I said.

Frustration was welling up in me, and Al could hear it in my voice. He never complained about the diaper disarray again after that.

Al arranged for a refrigerator to be delivered to our house. We didn't need it as much in the cool season, but we looked forward to having cold food and ice in the hot weather to come.

Ice cubes and crushed ice are decidedly American yearnings, we found. Cafés and restaurants in Greece served chilled, refrigerated drinks, but ice was never offered. Pepsi was the only American soft drink we could get. By the end of our tour of duty, my biggest craving was for a Coca-Cola with crushed ice.

Authentic Gypsies with beautiful, shiny black hair appeared at our door regularly. They were Romany people of a lineage widely disbursed over Europe. Greeks coined the name 'Gypsy', a short form of the word 'Egyptian', which some now consider derogatory. In the 1970s, Gypsies were the door-to-door salesmen of Greece.

We admired the Gypsies for their innate street smarts. They were well-groomed and nicely dressed. Their clothing was usually a little brighter than what the rest of our neighbors wore. If we didn't want to buy the unique wares the Gypsies brought to our house, they were up for trading, also. If all else failed, they asked for a hand out. This was all communicated by gesture and facial expression, since we only knew a few words of their language.

All the children, the Greek as well as the Gypsies, loved American chewing gum, and the adults coveted American cigarettes. Trading with the Gypsies became one of our favorite amusements, and we looked forward to their visits to our home.

Having no television to watch really frees up your day. Even with daily shopping and clothes washing, I had abundant time on my hands while Al worked his eight-hour shifts. We read almost every book in the detachment's library. Both Al and I wrote letters home each week, and our families wrote back. Thin, onion-skin letter paper that could be airmailed was used. We anticipated hearing news from our folks, but the letters took three weeks to be delivered. Packages took five to six weeks.

By the time Thanksgiving arrived, we began to feel a little homesick for our families back in the States. Thanksgiving isn't a Greek holiday, but we did see whole flocks of turkeys being herded down our street on their way to the Saturday street market around the square. The Americans celebrated Thanksgiving all together like a big family at the detachment's mess hall. The cooks really outdid themselves preparing the traditional feast of turkey and all the trimmings for us to savor.

They even baked pumpkin pies.

After Thanksgiving, we made a major supply run to Athens, and two of the American airmen went with us in our tiny Peanut car. The kids stayed in Kato with our friends, Mac and Roberta. This trip was made in the daytime, which afforded sightseeing along the way. I would compare driving the highway between Kato and Athens with traveling the Pacific Coast Highway along the California, Oregon, and Washington coasts in the US. Sheer cliffs dropped straight down to the sea, which was all shades of aqua, cobalt blue, peacock blue, and turquoise.

Many pretty villages were along the way. My overall visual impression of the villages was white stucco houses with blue or green shutters and doors. The towns seemed welcoming, tranquil, and slow-paced. The tables of sidewalk cafés were set up right on the edge of the highway with no curb to protect them.

Even though we were on a major highway, we still had to stop for herds of sheep and goats. Along the road, a rock outcropping jutting out over the water looked remarkably like the head of a sheep and was used as a landmark by the Americans. We nicknamed it 'Souvlaki Rock', a reference to the many lamb kabobs we all consumed.

We stopped for a Nescafé frappé at the popular tourist café in Corinth near the bridge that spans the canal. Corinth may sound familiar to the reader because in the Bible, Paul wrote two of his letters to the Corinthians. That connection makes you realize what an ancient country Greece is compared to America.

The Apostle Paul spent time in Athens 'reasoning' with the worshipers in the synagogue and with those who happened to pass him in the central marketplace. Paul found the Athenians very religious, but they were worshiping a myriad of gods, including one known as 'the unknown god'. The Stoic and Epicurean philosophers he met didn't understand what he tried to tell them about Jesus and the Resurrection, so they took him to Ares Rock to confer with the elders of the Areopagus, a council of learned men. Ares Rock is a low rocky hill northwest of the Acropolis.

The elders asked Paul what this new doctrine was. They wanted to know more. Paul stood there on the hill amidst the Areopagus and proclaimed that God created the world and everything in it, Jesus is our savior, and He has been resurrected after dying by crucifixion. Paul's speech is recorded in the Bible in Acts 17: 22-31 and on a plaque on Ares Rock.

Some of the elders wanted Paul to return and speak again, but he left for Corinth instead. He stayed there for eighteen months, working as a tent maker, spreading the gospel, and helping establish the church. Many Corinthians believed in Jesus and were baptized.

Corinth was the largest city in ancient Greece, much larger than Athens. Because Corinth controlled the harbors on both sides of the isthmus, the city became wealthy.

The Corinth Canal is mainly a tourist destination now. The four-mile-long canal is at sea level and is only seventy feet wide, but it is an impressive sight. It cuts through the Isthmus of Corinth and separates the Peloponnese peninsula from the mainland of Greece.

The huge project was attempted unsuccessfully in the first century AD. About fifteen years after the Apostle Paul lived in Corinth, the despotic Roman emperor, Nero, came there to personally break ground on the canal in 67 AD. His workforce consisted of about 6000 Jewish prisoners of war captured in Galilee. They were forced to dig by hand. The slaves progressed only about one-tenth of the way through the isthmus.

Inspired by the opening of the Suez Canal, a modern attempt was made in 1881. Americans don't think of 1881 as modern, but in a country as ancient as Greece, it was in the modern era. Many failures and bankruptcies delayed the digging, but it was finally completed in 1893. Even then, operational difficulties disrupted the use of the canal. Without locks, the currents in the canal were too strong at times to be navigable. The currents and frequent landslides down the sheer walls frustrated the canal's success.

At the end of World War II, the retreating Nazi forces intentionally blocked the canal with explosives and debris, and they destroyed the bridge over the canal. After the war, the US Army Corps of Engineers worked to reopen the canal by 1948. All that work was done so a few small crafts could take a shortcut. It did create quite a thrilling sight for the busloads of tourists, though.

Cue the music:
"Crystal Blue Persuasion"
Tommy James and the Shondells

We continued on to Athens or *Athena* as the natives call it. This visit we had a little more time to explore the city, mingle with the citizens, and relish the food. Athens is one of the world's oldest cities, having been inhabited for around seven thousand years. That is an astonishing seventy centuries. America is a pup compared to that. We explored the ruins and the streets of the *agora*, the ancient central marketplace where Socrates, Plato, Aristotle, and the Apostle Paul had walked, in the birthplace of democracy.

Athens had quite a growth spurt in the 1950s and 1960s. By the early Seventies, it was quite congested. We found it best to leave our Peanut car at the Hotel Kreoli and take a taxi to the Acropolis, the citadel in the center of the city.

Athens is bowl-shaped like Los Angeles and Mexico City, with a low center and hills rising around the outlying areas. This geography contributes to the smog problem that plagues all three of these cities. In 1971, the Greeks were worried the sulfurous emissions from factories and vehicles were beginning to erode their irreplaceable ancient ruins.

In 1975, after we had returned to the States, an ambitious restoration project began. The restorers even reassembled some of the columns that had been knocked down in the eighteenth century and put back incorrectly by prior curators.

As our taxi approached the Acropolis in the center of Athens, we saw the Parthenon perched atop the flat table rock mesa like an ornament on a wedding cake. The sunshine lit the white marble, making it look incandescent. The structure can be seen from all the outlying areas of Athens and as far away as the Port of Piraeus, the main harbor of Athens.

Some of the world's most wondrous archeological finds surround the Parthenon on the Acropolis, but they all pale in comparison. The colossal size and color of the giant marble columns is awe-inspiring. In 1971, visitors were allowed to climb over and through all the ruins, so of course we joined right in and did it, too.

We heard dozens of diverse languages being spoken by the tourists who were attracted to the site. Guides, fluent in many tongues, waited to be employed by the sightseers.

If someone forgot their camera, they could hire a photographer with a homemade box camera to create a black and white picture. The photographer covered himself with a black-out cloth before exposing the glass plate inside the camera. The pictures had a beautiful silvery quality unmatched by modern digital cameras, and they came out looking a hundred years old.

We scrambled up and down the Acropolis, exploring the ruins. We sat in the Amphitheater of Dionysus in marble seats and pretended we were the erstwhile citizens of Athena watching a play.

Near the Parthenon, we beheld the Porch of the Caryatids, the 'babes' of the Acropolis. The six sculpted women with braided hair and draped gowns served as columns to hold up the portico roof of the Erechtheion on their heads. They were built to bear the heavy weight, but they are still well-proportioned with slender necks. Most are missing their noses and hands, which have worn away or broken off through the years. The building attached to the porch has been used to house sacred objects, as a temple, and legend has it, to house a Turkish harem.

The Erechtheion was destroyed during the Greek War of Independence. The structure we saw had been reconstructed.

A Scottish nobleman, Thomas Bruce, the seventh Earl of Elgin, was an ambassador to the Ottoman Empire from 1799 to 1803. He arranged for artists to be allowed to sketch the sculptures and edifices on the Acropolis. By 1801, his crew was beginning to take castings and remove loose stones. This was probably accomplished by bribery.

By 1803, Lord Elgin had accumulated a ship's cargo of artifacts, including one of the caryatids. He attempted to cart off a second statue with disastrous results. It broke into several pieces. Lord Elgin claimed he was only trying to protect and preserve the precious artifacts from the Turkish, who had no idea of their value and no regard for them.

Lord Elgin's ship left for the British Isles, but was wrecked, and the cargo was dumped in the sea. Divers spent about three years recovering the relics, and Lord Elgin spent a great deal of money in the effort.

He displayed the intact caryatid and many other relics in his mansion in Scotland. In later years, his need for cash prompted him to sell the caryatid and some other pieces to the British Museum, where they are still housed today. He sold them for about half what they had cost him, so the rumors that he made a fortune stealing from the Greeks are untrue.

In 1979, the Athenian restorers removed the remaining original caryatids to the Acropolis Museum for safekeeping and replaced them with replicas. I'm glad we got to see most of the originals in their places on the porch.

Lord Elgin's schemes actually did result in the preservation of the purloined artifacts. During World War II, the threat of German bombings prompted the British Museum's caretakers to move the collection underground to a defunct train tunnel. The difficult move was performed secretly with a great deal of care. The pieces remained there underground for about ten years. If the sculptures had been in Athens during the war, many probably would have been destroyed.

Recently, laser cleaning of the original caryatids in Athens was begun with great success. Layers of grime built up over centuries have been painstakingly removed, leaving the first caryatid looking as immaculate as she did the day she took her place on the Erechtheion porch. The color of the unsoiled marble is ivory and pale apricot. Each of the five statues will go through the laser process, taking six to eight months to complete. Museum attendance is up. Everyone wants to see the ladies of the Acropolis looking so lovely.

Greek sculpture has been the epitome of the art form for centuries. The Roman conquerors brought back beautiful examples of Greek statuary and started a craze. Wealthy Romans wanted all things Hellenistic. More sculptures were desired than were available, so Roman sculptors, as well as a few Greeks, began copying the most popular pieces to fill the voracious need for beauty.

Some were exact, carefully-measured replicas. Others were patchwork amalgamations of several famous works of art. Museums today are careful to label copies as such. Top museums like the Louvre in Paris display many original Greek works. *The*

Winged Nike, commonly known as *The Winged Victory*, and *Aphrodite*, commonly known as *The Venus de Milo*, are found there.

Our climbing and exploring left us ravenous. We proceeded to the neighborhoods called Plaka and Monastiraki at the foot of the Acropolis to find a sidewalk café. This area was built near the ancient *agora*, the meeting place in the center of the city where Socrates and his student, Plato, walked among the citizens of Athens. No vehicles are permitted there, because the streets are only about ten feet wide and are even narrower in some places. The sidewalks, when present, are only one person wide, and all the square footage is utilized.

The exteriors of the cozy shops in the area had a veneer of goods for sale, ready to grab the attention of passing tourists. We saw handmade leather belts, bags, and sandals. Knitted, crocheted, and macramé items were popular.

We observed hippies wearing coils of hammered gold slave bracelets on their upper arms. The same styles graced the arms of the women of Athens of old to complement their togas. Many items for sale were decorated with the distinctive Greek Key design.

The instantly recognizable pattern of the Greek Key is associated with Greece by people around the globe. It has been used as a decorative border on pottery, architectural bas-reliefs, and marble floors during ancient times, and it is still hugely popular today. One modern New York City café is famous for their blue and white Greek Key coffee cups. The Greek Key motif never goes out of style. It is a classic that has endured for centuries.

We bought a bright orange Flokati rug to warm the cold floor of our house, and I got a fringed macramé and crocheted purse. Walking through this district bustling with pedestrians, it was not unusual to encounter a full scale archeological dig uncovering more ruins. Blasé Athenians strolled by without glancing left or right. Archeology is an everyday thing to them.

Many food vendors in the area only had a service window opening on the sidewalk, with a table or two set up for their customers. The fragrance of lamb and spices cooking over charcoal beckoned to us and aroused our appetites.

We dined on *gyros,* which are now commonly found in American cities. In the 1970s, we had never heard of *pita* bread. The flat bread was lightly grilled and filled with seasoned ground lamb slices. The meat was shaved from a large ham-shaped loaf cooking on a slowly rotating vertical spit. A garnish of tomato, onion, and *tzatziki* sauce made with yogurt, chopped cucumber, and mint was added. The *gyros,* as well as *souvlaki,* became our food mainstays. The food sold on the street and in the stalls was consistently good.

Souvlaki are one-inch cubes of lamb skewered and cooked over charcoal. The meat is marinated in lemon or lime juice, olive oil, oregano, and thyme to flavor and tenderize it. Lime juice is squeezed over the cooked meat moments after it is taken off the grill. A small bite of grilled bread is added to the end of the skewer.

Street vendors were found throughout the country selling *souvlaki,* the Greek version of fast food. *Souvlaki* has been consumed, with few variations, since Aristotle's day. It is even mentioned by Homer in his writings.

Souvlaki satisfied our carnivore tendencies. A popular side dish of fried potatoes with *moostardah* instead of ketchup as a condiment, often accompanied the kabobs. Yes, *moostardah* is Greek for mustard. I would not have thought it possible that we would live a year without ketchup, but we did, and we didn't miss it at all.

As the sun began to set, we looked up to see the Parthenon flooded with golden lights. The glow looked like an eternal flame burning in the heart of the structure.

We returned to our favorite hotel, The Kreoli, for a good night's sleep. The next day, we stocked up on supplies at the Air Force Base Commissary and set out for Kato. Every crevice of the Peanut was stuffed with diapers, food, and supplies.

The trip had renewed our spirits, as well as our supplies. Country people love to go to the city, and city people long for the country. It is human nature.

Approaching Kato in the dark, shooting stars engraved the black velvet sky. It felt good to be coming home.

Cue the music:
"Lucy in the Sky with Diamonds"
The Beatles

Our white-washed villa on a dirt road.

The Araxos radio shack where Al worked.

Matt, Tammy, and I with their stroller made for two.

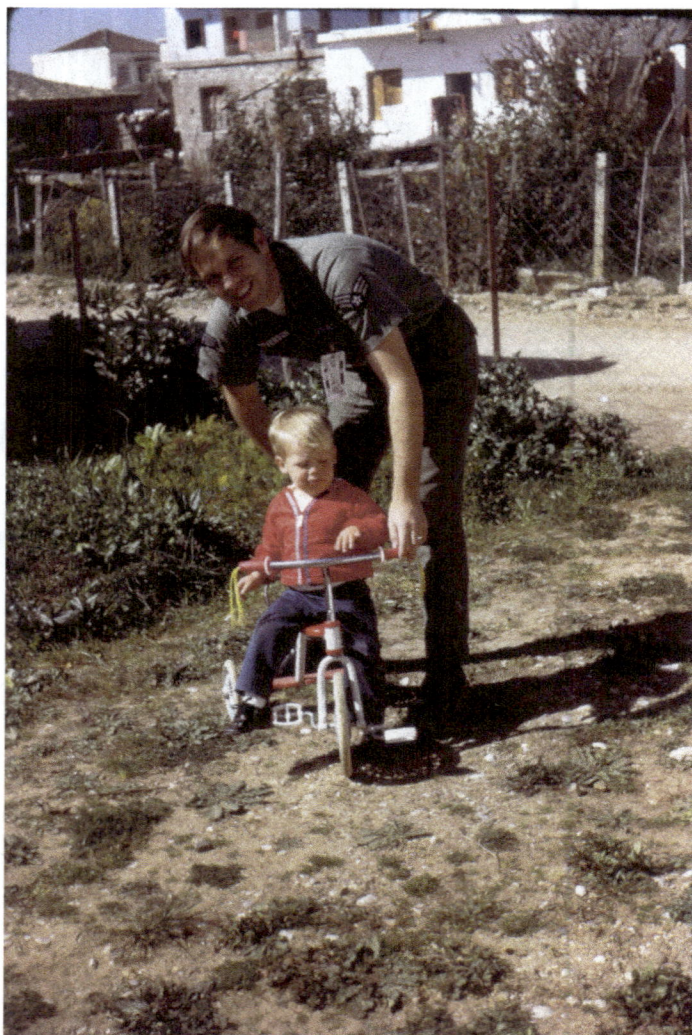

Al teaching Matt to ride his Greek tricycle.

Our landlord's mother with me and Matt.

A Kato man riding his burro.

Matt and Katarina playing ball.

The honey seller at the Saturday market in Kato.

Hanging out the washing to dry in our backyard.

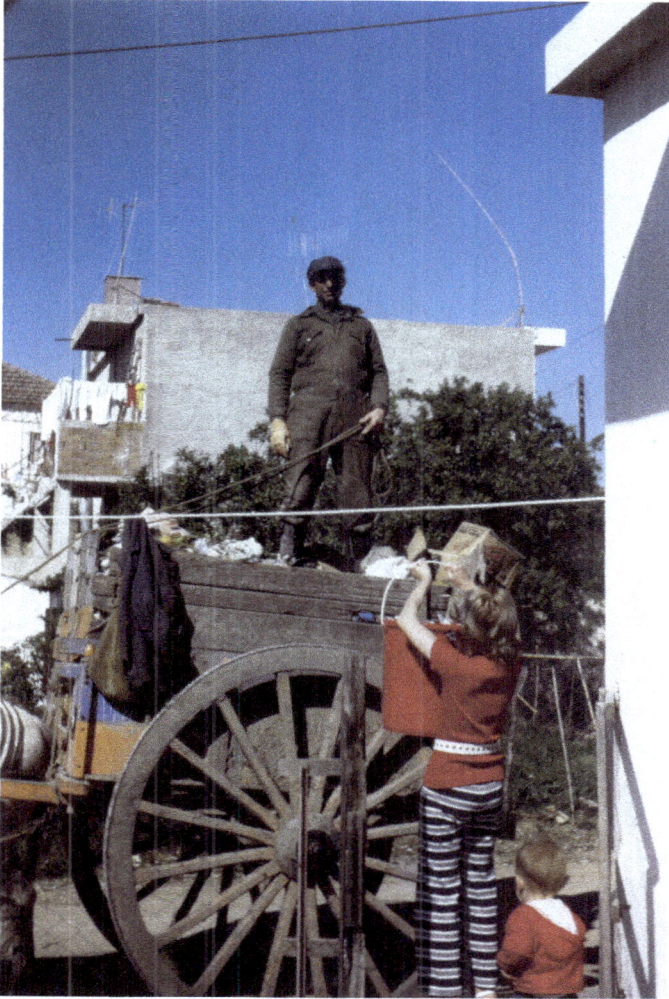

The trash collector visits our house.

The Kato butcher shop.

A typical kiosk in Patras.

A Gypsy child at our front door.

The bus station near our house.

Matt and I strolling by a donkey parking lot.

The fishmonger shows Matt a large catch.

The bridge to ancient Olympia.

Al and Matt at the ancient Olympic stadium entrance.

Matt and I rest on a column section at Olympia.

Gypsy girls.

Screaming Mimi at the Araxos Detachment fence.

A Greek woman on her way to the bakery.

A flower-covered float in the Patras Marde Gras parade.

A friendly frog at the Patras Marde Gras parade.

Girls on a Marde Gras float.

Matt and his friend Stacy pose with street vendors.

6 – MAMA TOLD ME (NOT TO COME)

The bleak rainy weather continued. Christmas came and went with little fanfare in Kato. It was celebrated very quietly with no decorations, lights, trees, or Christmas carols. For the Greeks, Christmas was a religious holiday only, without the secular trappings we Americans adore. No Santa, no elves, no tiny reindeer with red noses.

Our families sent gifts from home and asked us to wrap them in Christmas paper, not realizing that no such thing could be found in Kato.

We celebrated anyway. On Christmas Eve, our family sang "Silent Night". On Christmas morning, Tammy got her first doll, and Matt got a Greek tricycle with handlebar streamers. He had been missing the trike he left behind back in the States. He rode his new tricycle all around inside the house, singing a rousing rendition of "Jingle Bells".

We quietly rang out the old, worn-out, unfashionable 1971 and rang in the shiny new, state-of-the-art 1972. The New Year was a leap year, and it would be the longest in history, due to the addition of two leap seconds with the extra 366th day.

Al had to work a twelve-hour shift on New Year's Day, but he got to listen to football patched through on Armed Forces Radio from Brindisi, Italy. He heard the University of Oklahoma beat Auburn in the Sugar Bowl.

On less exciting days, we played Yahtzee at our kitchen table with homemade score cards. Al had managed to scrounge together five dice from somewhere.

I figured out how to make fried fruit pies in a skillet, since we couldn't bake anything. They became quite popular with our American friends.

Sometimes we had as many as eight people bellied up around our kitchen table, dining on our mismatched collection of plates. Whenever we had an abundance of any food, I would make big batches to share.

During the cold weather, I cooked big pots of chili. In the summer, I fried many skillets of okra, a great favorite. Some of the American airmen who weren't from the South had never heard of okra.

"What is this wonderful stuff?" our friend, John, asked me as he sat at our kitchen table.

"It's fried okra," I explained. "I guess you don't have it back home in Maine. It's a Southern thing. I think slaves brought the seeds from Africa."

"Good thinkin' on their part. Can I come to dinner tomorrow night, too?"

By the end of the season, our Yankee friends knew okra, loved it, and wondered how they had ever lived without it.

One evening, overcome by the blahs, Al and I decided to check out the Kato movie theater we had heard about. We got a sitter and walked across town to the storefront movie house. We paid a few drachs and went inside. Makeshift odds and ends chairs were set up in rows, and the projector stood in the back of the room.

We found what looked like good seats, but we wondered why everyone else was clustered together so closely in the center of the room. The lights went off, and the film began.

"Hey, this looks familiar," I whispered to Al.

It was an American gladiator movie made in Italy. I had seen it ten years before in 1962 in my home town. The English dialogue was now dubbed in Italian with Greek subtitles. I still remembered most of the story, so I filled Al in.

"It's 'The Magnificent Seven' done gladiator style."

The Spartans really kicked butt. The Greek movie goers were

obviously reveling in rooting for their local team.

As the film played on, we got colder and colder. We began to realize the Kato natives were grouped around a wood-burning potbelly stove for warmth. Shivering, we left before the end of the picture and never went back again.

The combination of the damp weather and the kerosene heater at home caused the whole family to come down with bad chest colds. We coughed and hacked for about two weeks. Just when we thought the worst was over, we heard Tammy make an odd sound after she had been tucked into her crib for the night. I rushed to her side and found her convulsing with her eyes rolled back.

I know now that convulsions are not uncommon when a child's temperature spikes quickly, but in 1972 I was a new mom with no knowledgeable grandmother around to help me. Tammy was only nine months old, and she was too young to tell me how she was feeling.

I grabbed her from her bed and touched my cheek to hers. She was burning with fever.

"Al, get the doctor!" I shrieked.

Without a word, he grabbed our phrase book and ran out the front door into the dark street. He sprinted to the bus station to find our landlord. The frantic look on his face alone probably told the man what he needed to know. Al pointed to the word 'doctor' and tried to pronounce the Greek version, *iatros*. He made a cradling motion with his arms.

Comprehending immediately, our landlord bolted out the bus station door with Al close behind him. The two men raced a block farther down the street in the opposite direction from our house. The landlord pounded on a door, rousing the doctor, and explained in Greek that our baby was sick. The doctor grabbed his bag and followed Al.

Meanwhile, I filled the bathtub with a few inches of cool

water and reclined our tiny child in it. She didn't like the chilly liquid and began crying robustly.

When Al and the doctor arrived at the house, the convulsions had subsided, but Tammy was looking alarmingly red in the face. The doctor, not used to treating such fair-skinned children, was concerned about the redness.

"*Patra,*" he said, pointing in the direction of the city. "*Nossokomio.*" Then he translated his own word in near perfect English. "Hospital."

When he realized we understood him, he drew us a simple map to direct us to the Children's Hospital in Patras. We loaded the family into the Peanut and rushed there. The normally short trip seemed to take forever.

At the hospital's emergency entrance, we were greeted by a group of caring professionals dressed in traditional white nursing uniforms and caps. They did not speak English. Tammy was taken to an examination room. Al, Matt, and I were left in a waiting room to worry and wonder what was going on.

After about an hour, a doctor came to us, holding a Greek to English medical translation book. As she approached we stood up, anxious to find out what was wrong with our baby.

She pointed to the Greek words, which translated 'scarlet fever'. I immediately began crying, my legs turned into noodles, and I started to faint. Al tried to support me while holding Matt, as well. I knew scarlet fever was a serious childhood disease that was contagious, so Matt would probably get it, too.

My hysteria caused the doctor to realize she had pointed to the wrong word.

She said, "*Ochi, ochi . . . bron-key-tees.*" She said it two more times, and I slowly began to understand. She had meant bronchitis!

The adrenaline rushing through me subsided, and peace washed over me. It felt like the calm after a violent thunderstorm on the plains of Oklahoma.

Tammy spent five days in the children's hospital with a nurse by her side at every moment. The hospital lacked the latest equipment, but the hands-on care was phenomenal. My heart broke each time I saw her lying there in her little metal crib, looking so small. I reached through the bars, and she grasped my finger with her tiny hand.

We were extremely happy when we got to bring Tammy back home. As we drove to Kato, I kissed her downy head and her cheeks dozens of times, and I delighted in her sweet baby fragrance.

"Words just can't say how filled with joy I am today," I said. "I'm so glad our little girl's okay."

"I hope we never have to go through anything like that again," Al added.

I try not to be superstitious, but I think his words may have jinxed us.

It wasn't long before Tammy was thriving again and pulling up in her crib. She was getting ready to take her first steps.

A few days later, I took a serious misstep. I was visiting with my neighbor across the fence while holding Matt balanced on my hip. I stepped back into a six-inch-deep hole, which I hadn't noticed was there. Carrying the extra weight caused something in my foot to tear. It was morning, and Al had just left for his shift at the detachment.

An hour later, I knew something was definitely wrong. As the day crept by, my foot and leg began to swell. The pain got worse. I usually have a high pain tolerance, but this was excruciation. The only medicine I had was aspirin.

Soon I couldn't stand up anymore and had to scoot around the house on a kitchen chair. I would have given anything to be able to call Al on the telephone. In desperation, I called out to my neighbors, but no one heard me.

By the time Al finally arrived back home hours later, I was in agony. He fetched the local doctor again, who wrote down another doctor's name and address in Patras.

We went by taxi this time, so Al could help me stabilize my leg, but I felt every bump in the road. In about twenty minutes, we arrived at the doctor's clinic, which was full of patients, even though it was late afternoon. Seeing I was in intense pain, the doctor saw me immediately. We later learned he was one of Greece's foremost foot doctors.

After x-rays, he diagnosed me as having a torn ligament. The physician applied a cast from my toes up to my knee to immobilize my foot and handed me a pair of crutches. His bill, including x-rays, cast, and crutches was fifteen American dollars.

I wore the cast and hobbled around on the crutches for six weeks. It was challenging to keep up with the kids, the shopping, and the laundry with the plaster on my foot. At the end of six weeks, I removed my own cast with a serrated kitchen knife. I felt like I was being released from prison.

Cue the music:
"So Far Away"
Carole King

We usually drove the Peanut when we went to Athens for supplies, but once we decided to take the train. We thought it would be an adventure for the whole family.

Al had ridden passenger trains as a child in Texas when he visited his grandparents. I had never experienced train travel. All I knew of it came from old movies I'd seen.

We realized we wouldn't be able to carry as many supplies back, but we were excited about the trip. Now that everyone was feeling well, we wanted to take the kids to see the sights of Athens. We knew they probably wouldn't remember the trip at their young ages, but we would take their pictures at the famous sites. Some day in the future, they could look through our photo album and think, *Yes, I was there.*

We parked the Peanut at the railroad station in Patras, purchased our tickets, and boarded the train. It looked exactly like those I had seen in old western movies. The rails were narrow gauge, which are less expensive to build. The cars were constructed mainly of wood with metal frames and wheels.

Inside, the seats were slatted wood similar to the benches we had seen inside the train station. We took off our jackets and sat on them for a little padding. The trip would take about six hours, which was two hours longer than it took by car. The train car began to fill with passengers until it was about two-thirds full. It wasn't uncomfortably crowded. We always welcomed the opportunity to people-watch in close quarters, without being obvious. The passengers looked a lot like our neighbors in Kato.

The train lurched and then began to move forward. The four of us looked at each other and smiled. Matt began to clap his hands in joyful excitement, and then Tammy followed his lead. She was learning from her big brother.

"We're on our way," Al said.

The train had a rhythmic rock and roll motion. Before long, the kid's eyes got heavy, and they both began to nod off. Train travel of that era was hugely agreeable to babies. It was like being rocked in a cradle for six hours. Adults were better off if they relaxed and let their bodies roll along with the movement of the train.

We saw different views of the small villages we had passed through numerous times by car. Some of the towns were whistle stops. If passengers or freight were waiting to be picked up, the station master signaled the train, and it stopped.

Al appreciated the freedom to look around and let someone

else do the driving. The scenery was impressive. The rocky hills were on our right, and the sea was on our left. We passed through some narrow mountain gorges and a tunnel. The train crossed the railroad bridge over the Corinth Canal, giving us an amazing view.

The other passengers sat quietly or spoke in soft voices. They were courteous to all those aboard.

We didn't bring any snacks along, so by the time we arrived in Athens, we were getting hungry. The train station was centrally located. We found a stand selling *gyros* and fried potatoes nearby. We dined at a sidewalk table and afterward found a taxi. We headed for our old favorite, The Kreoli Hotel, to relax for the night.

Early the next morning, we breakfasted in the hotel dining room on starched white table cloths. Then we put on our jackets and found a taxi to take us to the Acropolis. The sky was sunny and clear. It would be a good day to take the photographs we had planned. Our camera was an old Argus 35mm, which Al had owned since he was a boy. He used Ektachrome slide film, which produced spectacular colors.

We managed to convey to our cabbie, using pantomime and our limited vocabulary, that we wanted to take a family picture with the Parthenon in the background. By luck or design, he selected the Philopappou Hill. It was the perfect setting for our photograph.

At the foot of the hill, we found an unusual jail called the 'Prison of Socrates'. The cell was made by placing bars on the opening of a rocky cave. The barred windows and doors looked out onto the pathway.

Legend has it that Socrates, the father of Western philosophy, was imprisoned there when he became the stinging 'gadfly', as his student Plato recorded it. Socrates was what we would term a 'street-corner' philosopher. He was a stonecutter by trade who became a teacher without a classroom. He walked around Athens and talked to those who congregated. He devised the Socratic method of asking a series of questions, which provoke discussion and critical thinking, thus coming to a logical conclusion. The method is still used today, primarily among trial lawyers.

Socrates had a strong sense of fairness, and he upset the status quo in Athens. He irritated some powerful citizens, and I think he enjoyed doing it. Plato recorded Socrates saying that the upper echelon were sluggish and needed to be bitten like a gadfly bites a horse. He thought the 'biting' would provoke them to self-examination. Socrates was tried and found guilty of corrupting the youth of Athens and disbelieving in the ancestral gods.

While imprisoned, Socrates' best friend Crito tried to convince him to bribe the guards and flee to northern Greece. He offered his money and assistance, but Socrates was resolute about accepting his punishment.

Eventually, the day of Socrates' execution dawned. Surrounded by his students, he willingly drank the poison hemlock he was offered. He walked around the cell supported by his followers. When his legs gave out, he laid down. The poison worked its way to his heart, and he died.

Historians haven't been able to prove for sure Socrates was jailed there at the foot of the hill, but I believe he was.

Socrates never wrote down any of his ideas, but his brilliant student, Plato, faithfully recorded his teacher's words. In turn, Plato instructed another prodigious thinker when Aristotle came to Athens from the northern Macedon region. The foundation of scientific observation was born in Aristotle. What a tremendous contribution these three Greek citizens have made to mankind.

Philopappou Hill is landscaped using irregular shaped

pieces of marble as cobblestones. Dimitris Pikionis, an architect, took on the landscaping project in the early 1950s. He gave a great gift to the people of Athens and their visitors. The landscaping blends seamlessly with nature, but enhances each unique view.

The hill is a quiet place where the only sounds heard are trilling birds, even though it is in the heart of one of the world's busiest and noisiest cities.

The trail, which wasn't too steep, cut through the pine trees. Step by step, we climbed higher. At the summit we found an awe-inspiring panoramic view of Athens. We were only slightly lower than the Acropolis mesa, and we could see all the way to the Port of Piraeus and the Mediterranean Sea.

A well-placed marble bench provided the perfect place to pose the family. A friendly stranger snapped the picture for us. When I look at that snapshot today, it is the most iconic photograph we took during our year in Greece. Our little family is smiling, together on that bench with a sweeping view of the Acropolis as the background.

Philopappou Hill is known as the Hill of the Muses. I can understand why the mythical muses would like living on that particular hill. For thousands of years, muses have been deemed divine inspirers of poetry, literature, science, and the arts. We get our word 'museum' from the Greek word *mouseion,* meaning a shrine for muses. The mythic legends portrayed the muses as giving inspiration through the sounds of running water, the wind, or murmuring voices. Our words 'music' and 'amuse' come from the root word muse.

We descended Philopappou Hill and walked into the Monastiraki shopping district. We wanted to send each of our relatives a souvenir from Greece. Our rather lengthy list was organized by birthdates. We searched for a gift or two each time we visited Athens, starting with my brother's, who was a New

Year's baby. Next was Al's brother, who was a Valentine baby. We worked our way through the whole list eventually.

The Air Force Commissary was our next stop. We had purchased some large shopping bags in downtown Athens, which we could carry back on the train. They filled up quickly with necessities.

That evening, we dined at the Athens NCO Club. We were surprised to see it was decorated like a Las Vegas Casino and had slot machines. We played a few one-armed bandits and polished off a nice thick beef steak.

The next morning, we headed for the train station with our arms laden with paraphernalia and shopping bags. We got there early, boarded the train, and sat waiting to leave for quite a while. We had been warned that the time schedules weren't exactly set in stone. We didn't want to risk missing our train. Being late getting back to the detachment would have gotten Al into serious trouble.

The train finally pulled out of the station, and the familiar rocking motion began again. We left the busy city behind.

The return trip was restful and uneventful, except for one thing. We heard a strange noise and noticed one of the passengers had a shopping bag like ours, but her bag was moving and grunting. A tiny piglet peeked out of the top. We all laughed at the cute little pork chop. Al still talks about 'the lady with the pig in her purse'.

Cue the music:
"Peace Train"
Cat Stevens

Toward the end of January, a carnival with a few rides came to Kato. The American airmen jumped at the chance for some diversion. They turned out to ride the Tilt-A-Whirl and the bumper cars. In high spirits, they rammed into each other with their brightly painted cartoon buggies. Seeing big guys driving tiny jalopies was hilarious, but then we noticed the Greeks weren't sharing the joke.

They had turned out in their best clothes to drive the bumper cars in an orderly way, like they were driving a family car around the town square. Wearing their sport coats with their arms around their girlfriends at their side, they despised the American GIs for crashing into them. The owner of the ride concurred and ejected the rowdy Americans.

Without television to while away the hours, we seemed to always be looking for something to do. You can play only so many games of Yahtzee.

Al heard about a parade held each year in Patras before Lent, so even though it was a rather bleak and raw day, we decided to go. None of the other Americans wanted to make the trip, so we grabbed our coats and hopped in the Peanut. Within thirty minutes, we had reached the center of Patras. We found a place to park a few blocks from the parade route. As we walked down the street where the parade crowd had assembled, we saw a side of the Greek people we had never seen before.

A young man ran recklessly straight at us, springing along like a nervous gazelle. We recoiled, but not fast enough to avoid Al being thumped. A moment later, the bounder laughed hysterically and bounced on down the street.

"Hey, what was that?" I asked Al.

"That guy hit me on the head with a hammer!"

I laughed out loud. "Not a real hammer . . . a toy hammer, right?"

An instant later, I was showered with confetti. The usually sedate and dignified citizens were running around hitting perfect strangers on their heads with little plastic hammers and throwing confetti. The hammers made a funny sound, which implied your head was hollow. The parade-goers were absolutely giddy with excitement in anticipation of the parade starting. We were hit on the head and sprinkled with confetti several more times, and we all dissolved into laughter together. The parade was one of the highlights of our year in Greece.

Easter and the period prior to Lent are the most celebrated days for Greeks. The residents of Kato seemed brimming with happiness. Our next door neighbor brought us a beautiful Easter bread braided in a ring entwining red dyed eggs. The red dye represented Christ's shed blood, and the bread had been blessed by the priest. Other villagers brought us platters of delectable anise-flavored cookies.

The Greeks don't celebrate Fat Tuesday like they do in New Orleans. Instead, they have Burnt Thursday. Burnt refers to the grilling of meat. The Sunday following Burnt Thursday is the last day to eat meat before Lent.

The first day of Lent is called Clean Monday. Pans and utensils are scrubbed clean so that no trace of meat remains. During the forty days of Lent, the Greeks consume pure foods produced without the shedding of blood.

At one minute after midnight, Easter Sunday begins and breaks the forty day fast. A lamb roasted on a spit is the traditional Easter celebratory meal. Many Greek families eat at their outdoor tables laid with starched white tablecloths. The week before Clean Monday is the time for parades and parties.

The carnival parade we saw that day had elaborate floats worthy of the Rose Parade in California. Every inch of their display was carpeted with colorful flowers. Some floats featured large papier-mâché figures like jumping dolphins and cartoon characters. Girls wearing beautiful costumes rode atop. Marching bands provided music.

Men wearing enormous papier-mâché heads walked through the crowd, shaking hands. Their garb extended their height to about eight feet. They towered over the throngs of parade-goers.

We saw no other foreigners at the parade that day in 1972, but today in the twenty-first century thousands of tourists travel to Patras for the parade each year. The Patras Carnival Parade is known as one of the world's top three Mardi Gras parades, surpassed in size and attendance only by the parades of New Orleans and Rio de Janeiro.

Just a few weeks later on March 25th, we witnessed another splendid parade. This one was in our town, Kato. The parade marked the Greek National Day, which commemorates the day when Greece was finally recognized as an independent nation in 1832 after centuries of oppression by the Ottoman Empire.

From 1458 to 1832, Turkey occupied and ruled Greece. Greeks tried and failed many times to achieve independence. The final conflict lasted eleven years and reduced the Greek population by about two-thirds.

At the beginning of the war, which is known as the Greek War of Independence, Greece claimed approximately 2,500,000 citizens. By 1832, only about 800,000 endured. The Peloponnese peninsula, where our town, Kato, was located, acted as the heartland of the revolt. Self-appointed insurgents called Klephts fought valiantly to regain their independence and were able to control the countryside, while the Turks holed up in the fortress above Patras.

The traditional Greek male ethnic costume is derived from the Klephts uniform. It consists of a pleated kilt, a bolero or a waistcoat depending on the weather, and white wool tights. Klephts wore a fez-like red tasseled hat and red clogs with black pompons, which are also part of the outfit.

Each pleat of their kilt represents a year under Ottoman occupation, so each kilt should have three hundred and seventy-four pleats. Most modern men would find this uniform cumbersome, but it was lightweight and manageable compared to the clothing worn in that day. The Klephts took great pride in their uniform, and so did the revelers at the parade in Kato one hundred and forty years later.

The female national costume can be traced back to Queen Amalia, who reigned with her husband, King Otto, from 1832 to 1862. She came to Athens from Germany and was an immediate trendsetter. She realized that wearing the latest Paris fashions probably wouldn't endear her to the rustic people she ruled.

She created a garment, which is still known as the Amalia dress today. It consists of a loose-fitting white cotton or silk blouse under a richly-embroidered midnight blue or burgundy colored vest or jacket. She wore an ankle-length unpressed pleated skirt, usually a light sky blue color, and a soft cap with one long gold tassel. The queen and her ladies-in-waiting all wore the outfit, and it soon became quite popular with the women of Athens.

The number of marchers in the parade that day swelled the population of Kato to three times its normal size. Troops of children, arranged by age from six to sixteen, marched wearing their ethnic costumes. The parade started with the youngest group and progressed up to adults. All were in native dress.

Last came soldiers in modern military uniforms, displaying guns with bayonets and marching in formation. The march tempo music was broadcast over speakers. Bystanders, wearing their finest clothes, waved Greek flags and cheered as each group passed. Patriotism was manifested throughout the whole town. We Americans joined in. It felt good to stand up and cheer for our adopted compatriots.

The dismal winter with all its challenges began to fade into a more agreeable spring. Nights were still cool, but not bone-chilling cold. Days were brightened and warmed by sunshine. A sweater still felt good, but the possibility of balmy weather was in the air. The stores started having sales on heavy wool clothing, which gave us hope that winter was really over.

Winter released her icy grip around our hearts. As the season changed, our spirits began to warm and open like wildflowers.

Cue the music:
"I Can See Clearly Now"
Johnny Nash

7 - MORNING HAS BROKEN

Our plans for traveling around Europe were crushed like grapes in the wine press. The detachment was shorthanded, and the problem seemed to be getting worse each time an airman completed his tour of duty and departed. The radio section needed thirteen airmen, but was getting by with only six. We would not be getting our yearly thirty day leave, and Al would be on twelve-hour shifts indefinitely. We were determined to take as many day trips as possible.

Our next destination would be Olympia, the site of the ancient Olympic Games and the origin of the Olympic flame. We planned to make the 95 kilometer trip by bus, with the last leg to the consecrated site by taxi. We were forced to cancel our plans a few times due to rain, but finally the rain ended, and a beautiful spring day dawned. Tammy stayed home with the babysitter. Al, Matt, and I boarded the bus for Olympia. There were only a few passengers that day.

The bus followed the periphery of the Peloponnese. There weren't many villages between Kato and Olympia, so it was almost an express bus.

As we entered the countryside, my eyes searched for the first signs of spring. I was rewarded by the sight of hundreds of brilliant red poppies growing wild on the rocky hills. Sheep and goats grazed among them. Fuzzy newborn spring lambs and kids frolicked near their mothers. This was their playground. The tableau was like a painting, and it was a feast for my eyes after the long rainy winter.

In about an hour and a half, the bus approached Olympia, and we disembarked. There weren't many villagers around the bus stop. We went inside and purchased a guide book. Then we found a lone taxi cab, and Al asked the driver to take us to the original Olympic site. On the way there, we crossed the Kladeos River over a gracefully arched bridge. It was one of the most beautiful bridges I've seen.

The sacred grove had the countenance of a bride. Wild almond trees were veiled with fragrant white blossoms, and fields of white daisies encompassed the ruins. The area, wooded with cypress and aged olive trees between the confluence of the Kladeos and Alpheios Rivers, was like a haven. The cab driver left us there, and we were alone on hallowed ground.

No other tourists were there that day. Anything modern or noisy seemed out of place. The only sound we heard was made by honey bees buzzing softly around the almond flowers.

"It seems like we should be whispering . . . not talking out loud," I told Al. "I feel a presence here."

I felt a hushed reverence I've never experienced anywhere else, even in church or on a battlefield. I had no admiration for the mythical Greek gods who were worshiped there. I esteemed the athletes who made peace with each other and gave their absolute best to attain the ideals of virtue, physical strength, and beauty. They devoted themselves to win a sacred olive branch and honor for their home town.

"The guidebook says Plato, Aristotle, and Alexander the Great were here. Several Roman emperors including Nero came too," Al said. "Nero was a real bad guy."

"Yes, he was one of the worst. I've read that he used Christians as human torches in his palace garden."

The ancient Olympians were the professional sport figures of their day. They trained for ten months at home and then for one month in Olympia prior to the July games, which were held every four years.

Early games lasted just one day, but over the centuries the period was lengthened to several days. The foot race called the *stade*, from which we get our word 'stadium', was the only contest in the first thirteen Olympics. After that, more and more events were added, until there were over fifty.

The pentathlon consisted of running, jumping, discus and javelin throwing, and wrestling. Chariot racing was highly popular. Horse races had nude jockeys riding bareback. There were even competitions for poets, trumpeters, writers, and heralds.

Winners of the foot races would move on to compete in boxing, then wrestling, and finally *pankration. Pankration* was savage, no rules fighting, involving blows, kicks, strangling, and the twisting of limbs. When the weaker man admitted defeat, the winner would be named the champion . . . the original tough man. As victor, he would be lauded as *almost* a god.

Most champions were guaranteed free meals for the rest of their life. Only in Olympia was worship of mythic gods mingled with the honoring of flesh-and-blood athletes. The ancient games endured for over one thousand years, which proves their staying power. Even the Roman conquest of Greece in 146 BC served to strengthen the eminence of the games.

A great contribution to the success of the games happened in the 9th century BC. King Iphitos asked the oracle at Delphi what he should do to save Greece from ongoing civil wars and pestilence. She instructed him to reinstate the Olympic Games and declare a sacred truce for their duration.

The truce made the games accessible to all Greeks, since they could travel in safety to Olympia. The peace accord eventually made it possible for athletes and spectators throughout Asia Minor, Cyprus, and North Africa to participate. Truce breakers were punished harshly.

Cue the music:
"Aquarius/Let the Sunshine In"
The 5th Dimension

On that memorable spring day in 1972, we entered the stadium under the triumphal archway where thousands had gone before us.

"Look, Al. Here are the starting blocks. They're still here," I exclaimed.

"I'll race you," Al said. "Come on, Matt. Let's go."

We raced down to the finish line blocks, pretending we were competing with an imaginary crowd cheering us on.

The stadium could accommodate over 40,000 spectators seated on the knolls surrounding the field. I tried to imagine the scene back then. I visualized a modern track meet, but with all the onlookers wearing togas. In my mind's eye, I could see frenzied wagering, shouting, and cheering amongst the observers.

There wouldn't have been any slaves or women in the crowd, because they were forbidden to witness the competitions. Non-Greek men could watch, but could not compete. Contestants had to be free Greeks who had not committed a crime. Most of the competitors were nude. Several events might have been going on simultaneously. A three-ring circus comes to mind.

The rules for eligibility were bent for the despotic Emperor Nero. He competed in a ten-horse chariot race in 67 AD. He fell from his chariot and failed to finish the race, but he was declared the winner anyway. The year following Nero's death, his name was stricken from the list of winners.

The Greeks considered a fit and pleasant-smelling body to be both a work of art and an offering to Zeus. Before a competition, athletes bathed and perfumed their bodies. They, or their servant, applied olive oil to their skin, followed by a dusting of fine sand for protection from the elements.

After the contest, athletes, or their slaves, would scrape the oily, sweaty, and often bloody coating from their body with a small metal tool called a *strigil.* The scraped residue was considered a powerful ointment and saved for healing purposes.

Just outside the stadium's archway we saw sixteen empty pedestals.

"Look at this," Al said. "The guide book says each pedestal once held a bronze statue of Zeus. The figures were created with money taken from fines levied on cheaters. There must have been a lot of cheaters!"

"That was a not-so-subtle reminder to the athletes. If you cheat and get caught, you will pay," I observed.

"I thought the ancient Olympians had such high ideals. I guess someone's always trying to get away with something."

"That's human nature from 1972 BC to 1972 AD. I notice there's not a trace of the bronzes left. I guess they were melted down for scrap. What a shame."

Historians believe people began to gather at Olympia to worship Gaea, the mythical goddess of the earth and mother of the Titans. Most high school students in the USA have been forced to study Greek mythology, but find learning the stories from movies like *Clash of the Titans* more palatable. Unfortunately, the Three Stooges liked to take liberties with the myths, so if you relied on them instead of doing your reading, you probably failed the pop quiz.

The myths are primeval explanations of how the world was created, the meaning of life, and are, of course, for entertainment value. You have to admit the adventures of the gods, goddesses, and mythical creatures are sure enough creative.

The Olympians were the pantheon of twelve mythical gods and goddesses who ruled the world after defeating the Titans.

They were Zeus, king of the gods, Hera, wife (and sister) of Zeus, Poseidon, Hades, Hestia, Ares, Athena, Apollo, Aphrodite, Hermes, Artemis, and Hephaestus. According to the legends, the gods were interested in athletic games. Zeus wrestled, Apollo boxed, and Hermes ran.

The early Olympic Games were held to honor Zeus. A massive limestone temple, an altar, and a statue of Zeus were dedicated in the precise center of the sacred grove.

The ivory and gold statue of Zeus, who was represented sitting on an ornate ebony throne set with precious stones, was one of the Seven Wonders of the Ancient World. The statue was over forty feet tall. By comparison, the Lincoln Memorial in Washington, DC is half as tall.

Roman Emperor Caligula, who most historians agree was an insane tyrant, wanted to take the statue back to Rome. He also wanted the head lopped off and replaced with a replica of his own head. The ship dispatched to convey the gigantic work of art sank, so his plan was never carried out. It is believed the statue remained in place until around the year 393 AD, when it was taken to Constantinople (present day Istanbul, Turkey) and later destroyed in a fire.

The altar at Olympia was used to sacrifice one hundred oxen to honor Zeus during the games. A reference to those sacrifices is found in Acts 14:13 in the Bible.

Prior to the Olympic events, in which only men participated, girls competed in the Games Heraia in honor of their goddess, Hera. With their hair loose and wearing short knee-length tunics, local maidens ran a foot race. Their right shoulder and breast were bared.

The victorious runner won the right to display her image in the Temple of Hera. The image could be anything from a small token to a life-sized work. The winner would also receive a wild olive wreath and part of a sacrificed ox. The judges were sixteen women of the area who wove a sacred veil for the statue of Hera.

The Olympic flame still originates from the Temple of Hera months before the modern Olympic Games begin. The high priestess, now usually portrayed by an actress, lights a torch as it has always been done throughout the centuries. A curved mirror concentrates the sun's rays into its center and becomes hot enough to ignite the fueled torch. Backup torches are lit before that day, in case the sun doesn't appear. The burning torch is then taken to the altar, where it is used to light the first runner's torch.

Over time, many structures and facilities were added to the grounds outside the sacred area, or *Altis*. In addition to the stadium and the hippodrome, a gymnasium complex, guest houses for dignitaries, Roman-style baths, and offices for officials were built. Through the centuries, floods, landslides from nearby Mount Kronios, and powerful earthquakes have destroyed the structures and buried some under as much as fifteen feet of debris. Archeological excavations began in the 1800s and continued through the late 1950s.

Cue the music:
"Grazin' in the Grass"
The Friends of Distinction

That enchanted spring day, we walked through the ruined buildings. Zeus' Temple was once considered the most perfect example of Doric architecture. Now, its broken columns lay in rows on the ground like Oreos fanned out on a serving plate.

"Let's have our lunch right here in this field of daisies. This is a perfect place," Al said.

"Yes, it is. Everything here is broken and worn away by the elements, but still so beautiful. I love seeing all the subtle gradations of colors in the stones. The ruins seem like they belong to the earth," I added.

The field we chose to lunch in had once been an open courtyard laid with fine sand in the center of the gymnasium complex. Matt tumbled and played among the wildflowers where erstwhile boxers and wrestlers had sparred long ago.

Historians believe the last ancient Olympic Games were held in 393 AD. An edict around 381 AD from Roman Emperor Theodosius I prohibited all pagan rituals, even those practiced in a private home. He forbade all pagan festivals, which included the Olympic Games.

The worship of the mythical gods was deeply ingrained in ancient Greek life. Most homes had a statue of Zeus placed near the front door as a protector to ward off evil from the household. More humble dwellings had a small icon, which would be touched upon entering and leaving.

Imagine the chaos created by Theodosius' edict. Village magistrates were charged with enforcement of the anti-paganism laws, some of which were punishable by death.

Temples were destroyed, holidays abolished, and certain practices, such as divining by animal entrails were forbidden. Supposed 'eternal' flames were extinguished. Pagan amulets were traded for Christian crosses.

Olympia fell silent and virtually empty for the next fourteen centuries until 1827, when archaeologists from France arrived.

Our neighbors in Kato seemed superstitious, just like most Americans, but about different things. I'm sure some of their beliefs had pagan roots.

Most Greeks carry a small talisman at all times. It cannot be purchased. It must be received as a gift. It could be anything from a tiny gold pomegranate charm, the pagan symbol of prosperity, to a simple clove of garlic, believed to ward off evil. Cactus was often planted near the front entrance of the houses, which could actually ward off an unsuspecting burglar in the dark of night.

Some Greeks believe in the 'evil eye'. If someone looks upon you with envy, you can catch the evil eye. You will feel bad spiritually, as well as physically. To avoid the evil eye, believers wear a little blue marble with an eye painted on it, or a blue bracelet. They have great faith in the magical properties of the color blue. Garlic also is an evil eye repellent.

I didn't know until after we left Greece that blue-eyed people are thought to be givers of the evil eye. Our whole family has blue eyes, but our neighbors never seemed fearful of us. I guess they weren't among the superstitious.

We saw some of the elders of the community perform a strange spitting ritual. They would spit three times quickly, I assume to chase away bad fortune of some kind. People the world over have quirky customs and beliefs. It must be the latent juju gene in all of us. Scientists haven't mapped that one yet.

Cue the music:
"Behind Blue Eyes"
The Who

After our lunch in the daisies, we walked to the museum nearby. Constructed in 1886, it houses the most important archeological finds of ancient Olympia. Entering the foyer, we saw busts of the two archeologists who devoted their lives to excavating Olympia. Both were recognized by Greece for the priceless service they performed.

Next, we saw an architect's model of the Olympic site as it was before the devastation. We then proceeded into a repository of the finest examples of Grecian and Roman statuary. Most were chiseled from marble, but some were mere terra cotta, which have astonishingly survived over 2,500 years. I have trouble getting a terra cotta flower pot to last from one season to the next. Few bronze pieces have survived. Most of them were melted down centuries ago.

The human and animal figures from the pediments of Zeus' Temple were arranged in formation, just as they had been above the worshipers entering the temple centuries before. I was struck by the huge task the archeologists performed. Many figures had broken into multiple parts and been restored, using metal bars to connect where chunks were missing.

The Roman emperors, not known for modesty, were well represented in the statuary. Octavius Augustus was depicted two and a half times larger than life-size. One of the most memorable sculptures was an immense bull in the center of one hall.

The sculpture I found most beautiful was *Nike, the Goddess of Victory*, even though her face, wings, and several other appendages were missing. A small, but exquisite, plaster reproduction next to the ten-foot-tall statue showed her as she was before the damage. The artist who created her portrayed the feeling of flight. Leaning slightly forward, Nike appears to be just lifting from earth to fly away.

Excavations of Olympia turned up the sculptor Pheidias' workshop. A drinking cup was found with the words 'I belong to Pheidias' stamped into it. The cup and several sculpting tools were on display in the museum.

Each piece the sculptors chiseled expressed their worship for ultimate beauty and power, whether the subject was human or a mythical figure. I feel fortunate to have viewed their masterworks.

A few weeks before I wrote this chapter, I was surprised to hear a news report about the armed robbery of the antiquities museum in ancient Olympia. This was not the museum we visited on our trip in 1972, but a second newer museum, which mainly showcased objects, rather than statuary.

Two thieves took advantage of the one hour period between shift changes when the museum was guarded only by an electronic alarm. They disarmed the alarm, smashed a window, and were waiting for the sole female guard to arrive for her shift at 7:00 am.

They asked her for specific items, some of which were not found in that museum. When she wouldn't assist them, they gagged and bound her. The burglars got away with seventy-seven items, including a gold ring from around 1200 BC and an oil jar from 400 BC. These objects are priceless, of course. The bungling bandits destroyed a few items in their haste. It reminds me of the heist in the movie *Topkapi*, but without all the lovable characters.

Interpol has cataloged the stolen antiquities to prevent resale. The thieves' requests for certain items makes me wonder if the scoundrels might have been 'shopping' for an unnamed collector, rather than just stealing items they could fence in the underworld of Europe.

The financial dilemma currently hitting Greece has caused hundreds of guards to be laid off, leaving museums' contents vulnerable to opportunists. It troubles me to think of the noble and peaceful people I knew enduring rioting in the streets. From my point of view, I think the citizens would have better lives with less government. The European Union has not been a good fit for Greece.

Late in the afternoon, we boarded the bus for our return home. We rode quietly, etching all we had seen on our memories.

Cue the music:
"Stairway to Heaven"
Led Zeppelin

8 - TINY BUBBLES

On May 1st, one of our kind neighbors brought us a beautiful bouquet of flowers. That was a May Day custom in America when I was a child. We would secretly tie nosegays on our neighbor's doorknobs and run away.

The pretty spring weather enticed our family to take several trips to Patras for shopping and strolling the lovely city squares. In May the temperature was a copacetic seventy-five degrees Fahrenheit.

Our favorite place to linger was the Trion Symmahon Square, which honors England, France, and Russia, the three allies who helped fight for Greek independence. The square had a giant clock made of floral and foliage plants. The clock was a good landmark and a convenient meeting place. All the Americans knew where it was. It was within walking distance from the harbor.

The atmosphere of the square was enlivened by an old man playing a concertina, which looked to be older than he was. Round three-legged metal tables with chairs surrounding them were set up under the spreading branches of a shade tree.

Music is an integral part of American life. Our citizens are surrounded by the sounds of song on television, in movies, on radios in our homes and cars, on recordings of all types, and as background Muzak in stores and elevators. We enjoy lots of live music performances of every type, from Bach to Zydeco. PBS has introduced me to opera, and now I love it. Music pervades our lives.

I am amazed that all the wonderful music in our universe is made up of the same simple scale of seven notes, plus a few sharps and flats. The first of our ancestors to fashion a stick into a flute opened a rush of joy into the world.

Music was seldom heard during our year in Greece. I often wished I had my old transistor radio. We only heard music once in a great while, so it felt like a luxury when we did. When the old man played his concertina, it was like he had opened a jewel box and was sharing the treasure inside with us.

Seven musical notes, plus five sharps and flats, make all the melodies, and seven colors of the spectrum make all the myriad hues of our extraordinary world. The planet Earth spins in flawless mathematical synchrony, and God looks down at his creation and says, "It is indeed good."

Finding pleasure in small daily delights makes our lives blissful and brings us joy. Seeing a sunset, watching birds splash in a basin, or sipping a good cup of coffee are priceless moments. Such interludes are like fifteen minute mini-vacations, which rest and restore our minds.

In 1971, the first Starbucks had just opened in Seattle, starting a coffee revolution. Now I drink espresso as often as I can, but back in 1972, I didn't try it. The Greek coffee smelled aromatic, but looked thick like melted chocolate in tiny cups. We ordered Pepsi, instead.

"I wonder why you can't buy a Coke in this country," Al pondered as we sat and sipped our drinks.

"The Pepsi-Cola Company must have some special exporting arrangement with the government. I sure could go for a Coke right now," I said.

That craving would have to wait.

We dined occasionally in restaurants, instead of just buying food from street vendors. Kato had only one restaurant, but Patras had dozens from which to choose.

Usually, the restaurant owners motioned to us, inviting us to come right into the kitchen to show us what was on the bill of fare that day. Large pans of prepared food were on display, as well as raw meats and fish waiting to be cooked to order.

A feta cheese and spinach pie called *spanakopita* was popular. It was what most Americans would call a quiche. I was very fond of *moussaka,* a casserole of sliced eggplant, ground lamb, macaroni, tomatoes, onions, and cheese. The seasoning was cinnamon, which was unexpected and unique to our American taste buds.

Beautiful fresh seafood and Greek salad called *salata* were always good choices at every eatery. We noticed that the locals ate *salata,* bread, and olive oil at every meal. The simple, but delicious salads were sliced tomatoes, cucumbers, and onions dressed with extra virgin olive oil. Olives and cubed or crumbled feta cheese were served on the side. These healthy salads took only minutes to prepare. The vegetables were in the garden in the morning and on our plates by noon. The olive oil had such a delightful flavor that we didn't miss American salad dressing.

We found that olive oil was drizzled over all the seafood and vegetables, which made them very tasty. Naturally, we ate more of these healthy foods, because they were so delicious.

Scientific studies have recently shown that olive oil satiates hunger more than any other oil or fat used for cooking. Olive oil goes farther in recipes, also. Three-fourths of a cup of olive oil equals one full cup of butter.

The Greek diet has been proved to prevent heart attacks, strokes, and diabetes, and is believed to cut breast cancer and Alzheimer's risk quite dramatically. The olive is truly a gift from God.

For dessert we tried baklava, a honey-drenched pastry made of layered filo dough.

"I can see this would delight someone with a sweet tooth, but it's a little too rich for me," I said.

"Me too," Al agreed. "I'd rather have one of the Boston cream pies from the smoky bakery back in Kato."

"Maybe one of those little cups of strong black coffee is required to wash this dessert down."

The Greeks usually ended their meals with fruit. The sweet pastries were an afternoon snack for them and an occasional indulgence.

A Greek poet, Archestratus, was the first writer to treat cooking as an art. He wrote the precepts of gourmet dining in the fourth century BC. He called it *Gastronomia*, from which we get our word for the science of eating well, 'gastronomy'. Archestratus revealed his five golden rules, which are consistent with modern Greek cuisine.

Archestratus' rules included:
1) Use the highest quality and freshest foods.
2) Combine the ingredients harmoniously.
3) Use spices in moderation, in order that they
   do not overwhelm the ingredients.
4) Use light sauces.
5) Avoid hot spices and sauces.

No doubt, Archestratus would be surprised at the level to which gastronomy has risen in the twenty-first century, but would be proud the diet he espoused is considered the healthiest in the world.

The shops of Patras had trendy summer clothing, so we made a few purchases. By trial and error, I found I wore a size 41. One busy store sold only embroidered ribbons and trims. The large shop brimmed with thousands of patterns. I bought a few yards to decorate my jean jacket. I sewed it on by hand with a needle and thread. The Greeks seemed to love clothing decorated with colorful embroidery.

Patras, or *Patra* as the natives call it, is situated between the waters of the Gulf of Patras and Mount Panachiakon 6,319 feet above. The area has been inhabited for around four thousand years. The lower and newer section of the city is called Kato Poli, and the older upper section is called Ano Poli. The two precincts are connected by stairs. Above the city in the countryside is the Achaia Clauss Winery. At the top of the mountain are the ruins of the Roman fortification and the medieval Patras Castle.

Today Patras is Greece's third largest city with a population of nearly a quarter of a million people. The architecture is quite a mixture of styles. Americans like everything in their lives to be shiny, new, improved, and homogenized . . . just like their milk. Europeans like things left rough and natural. They favor allowing objects and structures to age gracefully without constant tampering. Throughout Greece, I noticed how integrated into their surroundings the oldest ruins seemed. It was as if the quarried stones had sprung up from the rocky soil like an organism.

The resistance movement of the War of Independence started near Patras, and the city was a bombing target during World War II. Wars and earthquakes have taken their toll through the years, so most buildings are relatively new. The Kato Poli, adjoining the harbor, was the first Greek planned community in modern times. The plan was created in 1829 and finally realized in 1858. Patras was the first city in Greece to have electric streetlights.

Patras is a busy port. Back in the 1970s, it was the place to catch a ferry to Italy or to the Greek mainland. In 2001, the Greek Constitution was amended to declare the sea strand a national treasure and the property of the citizens of Greece. No shops or other structures are allowed to block access to the shoreline. I'm not aware of a declaration of that type in any other country with coastal land. In fact, in the United States you might have to drive for miles and miles before finding a public beach. I'm glad someone went to bat for the Greek people on this issue. The coastline is one of their finest resources.

Right in the heart of Patras, you'll find King George I Square with its sparkling fountains. The square was included in the 1829 city plan, and the fountains cost seventy thousand drachmas each, a huge sum of money at the time. Great forethought by the designers made Patras a city with a quality of life comparable to the finest cities in Europe.

In King George Square, we found another photographer with a homemade box camera. I posed with the kids in front of one of the fountains. We had the black and white pictures made into postcards to send to our families back in the United States.

Cue the music: "You Showed Me" The Turtles

One winter evening, Al said, "Let's check out the night life in Patras. I've heard it's pretty cool."

We ended up in a cavern-like club on the edge of the old section of town. Watching the locals dance to European techno-pop music played on a jukebox was entertaining. A smog of cigarette smoke hung like a thick curtain in the room. The dancers were well dressed. They seemed to be a more sophisticated and cosmopolitan group than our neighbors in Kato.

The next morning, I felt like I had smoked a pack of unfiltered Camels from inhaling all the secondhand smoke. My lungs hurt, and my throat was scratchy. We went back to the club a couple times during the winter anyway, because we were bored and needed something to do.

Once or twice, we ventured into the Ano Poli section for shopping at a brass works. The Ano Poli was more of an industrial and warehouse district. We went there to buy some brass candlesticks to take home with us. The brass objects were remarkably heavy and well made. I still use the candlesticks I bought there.

Fine hand craftsmanship is greatly revered in Greece. Many craftsmen work alone or with only their close male relatives, which gives them the freedom to be their own boss. Independence seems to suit the Greek people. I can't visualize them being happy working in a factory with hundreds of employees.

Roman ruins of an *odeum,* a hall primarily used for music and poetry performances, and an outdoor amphitheater are found in the Ano Poli. These structures have been restored and are used for concerts and plays today.

Patras is famous, or you might say infamous, as the place where the Apostle Andrew was martyred. This happened about twenty-seven years after Jesus' resurrection.

Andrew and his brother, Simon Peter, were the first disciples to follow Jesus. Andrew met Jesus and went and told his brother, "We have found the Messiah."

The disciples followed Jesus until He was crucified.

After Jesus' crucifixion, the apostles were a group of frightened followers, hiding behind locked doors and fearing for their own lives.

But after the Resurrection and Ascension, they were convinced that Jesus was their savior and were willing to die for their beliefs. They faced violence and almost certain death. All but John the Revelator, the author of the Book of Revelation, died as martyrs.

Before Jesus ascended into Heaven, He said to his apostles, "Go into all the world and preach the gospel to all creation."

The Apostle Andrew was proclaiming the gospel of Jesus Christ around Patras in the year 60 AD. It is not known for sure what he did to anger the Roman governor who ruled over the region. The Roman conquerors were generally tolerant of those they reigned over, but some were much more dictatorial than others.

Some Bible scholars believe Andrew led a member of the governor's own household to Christianity. The apostle was arrested. He was given the choice to turn away from Christ, to worship the pantheon of Roman gods and the Roman emperor, or to be crucified. He was pressed to declare Nero as Lord and to offer incense to Nero and the gods. He refused to obey the Roman order and was crucified on November 30 in 60 AD.

Near the Patras harbor, he was hung on an X-shaped cross, rather than the Latin cross of Jesus. Andrew was bound to the timbers with ropes, instead of being nailed to them. The apostle was an old man, but he is said to have continued preaching to those who gathered around, until the moment he succumbed two or three days later.

The domed Basilica of St. Andrew was erected on the site where the crucifixion took place. St. Andrew is the patron saint of Patras, and a special ceremony is held at the site each November 30. A small finger bone, a skull top, and a piece of wood from the cross of St. Andrew are enshrined in the church. Mosaic art inside the temple depicts the crucifixion. The church remains an active center for worship today.

The Patras Castle Fortress was built high above the ancient city on an outlying hill in the 6th century AD. The location had been a strategic position overlooking the city since the earliest inhabitants arrived. Byzantine Emperor Justinian I ordered the castle's construction after an earthquake in 551 AD.

It was the custom of that era to incorporate spoils of war and fragments from previously ruined architecture into newly constructed buildings. The torso and head of a marble sculpture was added to the Patras castle as a guardian of the city and its citizens. The figure was called 'Patrinella' and was purported to protect Patras from disease and to shed tears when a prominent citizen died.

The fortress remained in constant use for the next thirteen centuries. It was triangular-shaped to fit on the outcropping hill. An inner and outer moat protected the citadel. Though besieged by a myriad of interlopers, it never fell until 1458, when the Ottoman Turks claimed dominion. It remained one of their primary seats of power in the Peloponnese.

During the Greek War of Independence, the Turks were surrounded by the scrappy Klepht independence fighters who tried repeatedly to storm the fortress. With the help of French allies, the Greeks finally drove the Turks from their stronghold in 1828. The long-fought independence came in 1832.

Cue the music:
"Here Comes the Sun"
The Beatles

Eight of us Americans decided to explore the Achaia Clauss Winery we had heard about.

"Let's pack a picnic lunch," I suggested to my friend Roberta.

"How about fried chicken like we have back home?"

Our group included our family of four, Roberta, her husband, Mac, their daughter, and a single airman friend of ours. The limitations of our tiny cars required us to take two vehicles. We loaded our lunch and headed up the hill about eight kilometers from the center of Patras. We drove through lanes edged with tall cypress trees. As we approached the winery, we passed rows of neatly manicured grapevines. We saw rust-colored tile roofs poking up above the tree tops.

Inside the secluded grove was a turret built of natural stone.

The castle-like structure had crenellated battlements at the top that looked like gigantic teeth with spaces between them. The tower reminded us of something from medieval England.

"Hey, this tower looks like it came straight out of a Robin Hood movie," Mac said. "Watch out for flaming arrows!"

We all looked up at the top of the tower, half expecting to see an archer drawing his bow on us. A carved sign above the arched entrance said the winery was built in 1861.

"Everything in this country is so old," said Roberta.

We always got a chuckle from Roberta's down-home comments. She was a country girl at heart.

I looked down the hillside at the vines. They looked almost over-pruned to me, but I have since learned that pruning is how the vine dresser produces the finest grapes. He removes all the grapes, except for four or five bunches. Then the plant puts all its energy into growing the remaining clusters. When ripe, the grapes must be picked by hand and treated very gently.

Gustav Clauss traveled from Germany to Greece in 1854. He came as a representative of Fels & Company, searching for possible products they might develop. When he arrived in Patras, he was particularly interested in black currants, a seedless berry that was already being successfully produced in the region. His diary says he discovered 'a paradise of vineyards' around Patras.

He took up residence and planted a few grapevines. His first wine was Mavrodaphne from a vine transplanted from an Ionian island. Gustav created the name which means 'black laurel'. He produced the sweet, full-bodied red dessert wine for his friends and himself. By 1859, Clauss and his partners decided to purchase land to establish a winery.

The first years were extremely problematic. On top of the laborious planting and building efforts, bandits arrived almost daily to steal whatever they could. Gustav persevered, and the winery produced its first Mavrodaphne and Muscat in corked bottles in 1873. I can't imagine a modern American business owner waiting patiently for twelve years to produce their first product.

Achaia Clauss Winery's Mavrodaphne has received rave reviews consistently through the years and has made the winery famous. Connoisseurs describe it as opaque and densely sweet with an enduring bitterness, which appeals most to the European palate.

The winery has had many eminent visitors, the first of whom was Elizabeth of Austria, consort to the Emperor, who arrived unexpected in 1885. That visit led to the custom of dedicating each barrel in the huge Imperial Cellar to a visiting dignitary. Composer Franz Liszt, astronaut Neil Armstrong, and Prime Minister Margaret Thatcher are among the celebrated visitors.

We walked in wearing shorts and hippie sandals where royalty had trod before us. We entered the first cellar through tall carved wooden doors. Row upon row of wooden casks awaited our inspection. They looked like enormous barrels lying on their sides in wooden cradles on the natural stone floor. The ends of the barrels were as tall as the men in our group.

Next we strolled into the Imperial Cellar, which contains barrels of every vintage, including the initial batch of Mavrodaphne from 1873. Two huge casks, which are twice as tall as a man, hold the 1882 vintage. That year's yield is considered the best ever produced. These rare Mavrodaphnes are released only for the most exceptional clients and the most momentous occasions. The cellar's contents are worth millions. The vats were so large, we could have used one as a garage for the Peanut.

Many of the barrelheads had elaborate carvings. The one I remember most was a full face portrayal of Dionysus, the Grecian god of wine and the grape harvest. With a naughty sparkle in his eye, he looked to be enjoying every swallow with gusto.

Wood barrels impart a unique signature flavor to the wine inside. Tannins are released from the wood, and a small amount of porosity allows some alcohol to evaporate. The small amount lost to evaporation is called the 'angel's portion'. The casks must be topped off from another barrel.

The process of making fine wine has been compared to giving birth. The grapes form and ripen on the vines for nine months, but that is only the beginning. Then the real artistry begins with knowing exactly which day to pick the fruit at the peak of sweet perfection.

A successful vintner must be a culinary master, a botanist, a chemist, and have a nose keener than a hunting dog's. He must have the taste buds of a gourmand and be strong enough to turn the heavy barrels. Having great intuition helps, too. Gustav Clauss seems to have been born with all these exceptional talents. The gifted winemaker died in 1908, but his German company continued to operate the winery.

During World War I, the Greek government confiscated the winery as an enemy alien asset and auctioned it off. A local currant grower named Vlassis Antonopoulos purchased the business and modernized the production methods. The Antonopoulos family sold the enterprise to Nikos Karapanos, the current owner.

Today Achaia Clauss Winery is the largest exporter of corked Greek wines. Some are robust, complex, and full-bodied, while others are more ethereal. A mélange of aromas and flavors give pleasure to aficionados, as well as occasional imbibers. The celebrated portfolio of thirty-two wines and four spirits are exported to forty-two countries worldwide.

The winery produces more than three million cases per year. That requires a lot of fruit, so the winery contracts with nearby growers throughout the Peloponnese. The present owner's praiseworthy goal is to keep production local and to preserve the historic Achaia Clauss labels and their superior quality.

Our informal guided tour trailed through the Imperial Cellar, the storage of the bottled wines, and wound up in the winery bar for tasting. The tables and chairs in the bar were made from wooden barrels, and the chandeliers were constructed of wine bottles.

I tasted the Demestica, a wine much maligned by snobs, but loved by everyone else. It was a light straw color with a slight peachiness. This summer wine was what I saw my neighbors bringing home in large, wicker-covered bottles. Demestica is still the world's largest selling Greek wine and is considered by many to be one of life's simple joys.

I purchased an unusual souvenir that day, which I still have. It was a tall tankard with an attached lid similar to a stein, but it was made of fragrant wood. No beer or ale was produced at the winery, so I came to the conclusion that it must be used for drinking Retsina, which Achaia Clauss did make at that time. Although I never tasted the Retsina, I imagined what a white wine infused with pine resin might be like. It would definitely be an acquired taste, but it is still popular today in Greece and a few other Mediterranean countries. Retsina is usually paired with garlicky and salty snacks.

Pliny the Elder, Roman writer and naturalist, wrote of using pine resin in wine in the first century AD, so we can conclude that Retsina has been produced for at least two thousand years. Resin was first used to seal the inside of porous amphora jars, so that oxygen wouldn't seep in to spoil the wine. Naturally, the strong-smelling resin flavored the wine.

By the third century AD, Romans had begun producing and using wood barrels successfully for wine storage, but Retsina had staunch fans by then. The name Retsina is protected by the

European Union and can only be used by Greek wineries. The modern Retsina is made to more exacting standards, resulting in a lighter, crisper flavor without the pungent whiff of turpentine some used to complain of.

One of the most colorful labels at the winery is on their Ouzo, which is a distilled spirit, rather than a wine. It shows a Greek soldier in the traditional Klepht uniform, wearing a snappy red fez and belt, white kilt and leggings, and a blue vest. Ouzo is known worldwide as a classic Greek aperitif, and production is restricted by the European Union to Greece and Cypress only. Most meals in Greece begin with Ouzo.

For centuries, *tsipouro* making was a ritual following the grape harvest. *Tsipouro* is also known as *raki* in Crete. The solids left behind after the pressing of the grapes were not wasted by the frugal Greek farmers.

The grape skins, seeds, and stems, the combination of which is known as 'the must', were left to ferment in vats. When fermented, the mixture was transferred to a large copper cauldron, which we would recognize as a 'still' or distillery. Closely guarded proportions of liquid, berries, spices, and aromatic herbs were added. The recipes were handed down from generation to generation.

When the concoction was brought to a boil, the vapors would rise to the top and be drawn off with copper tubing, creating a drip of clear spirit. Licorice-flavored anise root was a popular addition. This version of *tsipouro* eventually became known as Ouzo.

Ouzo production was given a big boost when absinthe, a drink nicknamed 'the green fairy' due to its grassy green color, was banned. Absinthe is another anise-flavored spirit that was embraced by the bohemian artists' and writers' culture of Paris in the late eighteen and early nineteen hundreds.

The French method was to drip the spirit from a carafe into

a glass over a special absinthe spoon holding a sugar cube. The sugar would melt into the drink. Absinthe contained wormwood oil, which was believed by many people to have psychotropic and addictive properties.

A few highly publicized crimes were blamed on absinthe imbibing. Although these conclusions were highly questionable, sales of absinthe were made illegal in 1915. Ouzo distillers stepped in to fill the gap and have continued to thrive.

Recent scientific tests of vintage absinthe have found nothing that would drive anyone to madness. Wineries were suspected of starting the absinthe rumors, but the Ouzo distillers were the ones who benefited most. Absinthe sales remained illegal in Europe until 2005.

Achaia Clauss Ouzo has the prominent anise flavor with hints of herbs, pepper, and lemon. American Ouzo drinkers have rated it as their favorite. Ouzo can be drunk as a straight shot, but it is most often mixed with water which causes the anise to be released and to 'bloom'. The drink becomes cloudy white with a faint blue tinge, and subtle flavors are liberated.

Today in Greece, Ouzo bistros called *ouzeris* are found in almost every city and village. These cafés specialize in serving Ouzo with strong-flavored snacks known as *mezes.* They are appetizers like fried calamari, fried sardines, olives, and feta cheese. Those who imbibe usually linger for several hours, sipping their Ouzo and sharing food with their friends.

During our year in Greece, I never saw anyone who appeared drunk. Greeks of that time viewed drunkenness as being disgraceful. Drinking on an empty stomach was known as drinking 'dry hammer' and was considered bad form. The Greeks around us in the 1970s drank alcohol in moderation to achieve *kefi*, a state of high spirits and relaxation.

After tasting the beautiful wines, we returned to our cars to retrieve our picnic lunch. We found a retaining wall under a sheltering shade tree and arranged our alfresco lunch for all to savor. Time passed as we frittered away the afternoon, casually nibbling on morsels and absorbing the great outdoors. The vantage point allowed us to see for miles.

Al pulled out his Argus camera and took a picture of our open air repast. When I looked at the snapshot a few days ago, it brought a memory of that extraordinary day. The remembrance was golden and filtered through the prism of a shining glass of Demestica. The men in our group were wearing sleeveless shirts and straw hats. The women wore soft hippie garb.

It occurred to me that our group looked remarkably like the diners portrayed by Auguste Renoir in his painting 'Luncheon of the Boating Party'. I was fortunate to see the painting when the Phillips Collection allowed it to tour middle America back in the late Eighties. The painting vibrates with life. You can almost hear the soft tinkling of the crystal wine glasses on the table and the murmuring conversations of the people around it.

The artwork depicts the carefree joy we felt that day at the winery. If Renoir had been with us there, I think he would have wanted to catch our likeness on his canvass and call it 'Luncheon of the Winery Party'.

Cue the music:
"Magic Carpet Ride"
Steppenwolf

9 – What a Wonderful World

The long summer days blended seamlessly, one into another. The temperature in Kato was around eighty-four degrees day after day, which was my idea of perfection. It was warm, but never hot enough to make you sweat. We spent that ambrosial season cherishing each other's company and all the life buzzing around us.

Many milestones were reached. Tammy learned to walk and soon after that to run. Matt got toilet trained, which reduced my diaper washing by half.

Most mornings, we all got up early with Al. We usually had fresh-squeezed orange juice, bread with honey, and sometimes an egg fried in olive oil for breakfast. Al took off for work at the detachment, and the kids and I would walk to town to do our food shopping for the day.

New vegetables and seafood were appearing in the market, and we were excited to have more variety in our meals. All the offerings were at their epitome of freshness. The tomatoes, okra, and shrimp were especially delicious. The vendors knew us and greeted us warmly. They competed for our business. A surge of goodwill engulfed us as we made our way down the main street in town.

The food was a great value for a tiny price. Most items were sold by the kilogram, which is the metric equivalent to 2.2 American pounds. I would say, *"Misso kilo,"* when I wanted half a kilo. Liquids were usually sold by the liter, which amounts to slightly more than our American quart.

I loved shopping for food in Kato. I never had an unpleasant experience. It was edifying for the soul, as well as the body. I can't say that about the modern American supermarket, although they offer a tremendous selection of goods brought from around the globe. Our local stores here in Texas are so busy they require parking lot traffic control.

Some mornings, the Kato fishmongers would have a prize fish set aside for us as a special treat. They had sea bass and mullet almost every day and shrimp sometimes. We learned the names of the foods we purchased most often.

Orange	*portokali*
Tomato	*domates*
Bread	*psomi*
Egg	*avga*
Cheese	*tiri*
Grapes	*stafilia*
Shrimp	*garides*
Beans	*fassolia*
Onions	*kremidia*
Carrot	*karote*
Spinach	*spanaki*

Though the vendors and I only knew a few common words, we communicated nonetheless. They showed me the way to clean and prepare the fish by acting it out. The ancient Greek mimes couldn't have done it better.

We always went to town on Saturday morning for the special market. Farmers and their wives would set up stands in the streets around the square. They brought animals, fruits, vegetables, and honey to sell. Balls of feta cheese about the size of a softball were sold nestled in handmade baskets. We all laughed when a woman held a small piglet by its back legs and walked it around like a wheel barrow. I never bought any live animals, though, because I knew they would become pets rather than dinner.

For lunch, I often made a simple dish of pasta, tomatoes,

and basil leaves with olive oil drizzled over it. We had sesame seed bread, too. I still love this meal. It's satisfying and delicious.

In the afternoons, Matt and Tammy played in the back yard while I did the clothes washing by hand in an old baby bathtub. The wringing was the most laborious part. I would hang each item up to dry with clothespins on the cord Al had strung. It wasn't long before the washing was dry in the warm breeze. The children liked to use the soap suds to blow bubbles with a wooden thread spool.

The kids had a few plastic toys we had purchased at one of the local stores, but Tammy preferred making mud pies with a few old jar lids from the kitchen. She decorated them with wildflowers. We should have had a clue she would grow up to be a talented pastry chef.

Matt loved to toss a ball over the fence to our neighbor, Katarina, and she would throw it back to him. At age nine, she was like a big sister with endless patience for our children.

Matt and Tammy had a bug collection, and a neighbor gave them a tiny pet duck that used the baby bathtub for a pool when I wasn't washing clothes. We adopted a stray puppy who wound up on our doorstep. He was named *Filos*, which means 'friend' in Greek.

I was raised as a 'free range' child. I was allowed to explore and learn without being overly supervised. At age six I walked to school and back home by myself. I got to use my dad's tools to make little projects. I gained a lot of firsthand knowledge about science and the way the world works. My childhood inspired creativity, and I learned to be self-sufficient. I tried to rear my children the same way.

We ate watermelon in the yard and had seed spitting contests. Our landlord's mother, garbed in her heavy dark clothes and headscarf, would come by to work in the garden plot and pick the produce and herbs. She smiled so big her eyes almost closed, showing her irregular teeth. She let the wildflowers grow naturally between the rows. I think she saw how much fun the children had picking them. She was a very sweet old soul.

I had purchased a plant with deep green shiny leaves at one of the Saturday markets, not knowing what kind it was. I simply felt the need to have some greenery in the house like I had back home in the States. It was planted in an old metal can. I would carry my plant outside each morning to let it get sunshine. At dusk, I carried it back into the kitchen and set it on the window sill. My next door neighbor, Katarina's mother, watched me do this day after day. Finally one day, she came over wearing her floral print house dress and apron. In her hand she carried some cigarette butts. I couldn't imagine what she wanted to tell me. She crumbled the butts and worked them into the soil around my plant.

I said, *"Nay, nay,"* meaning 'yes', to express that I understood.

After that, I saved the butts whenever a smoker visited our house and worked them into the soil. Around Easter, my plant burst into bloom. It was a gardenia with a fragrant white blossom that perfumed our whole house. Upon awakening to the lovely fragrance, I rushed over to show my neighbor. She taught me the secret for making gardenias flower, even though we couldn't speak the same language. Sometimes communication goes deeper than words.

Cue the music:
"For Your Love"
The Yardbirds

Life today in the twenty-first century has gotten extremely complicated. Most every item a consumer chooses offers endless options and specializations. The entire world is now our shopping mall. Some people get so bogged down by the plethora of decisions and weighing other people's reviews, they shut down altogether and can't choose anything.

For many years, I worked in our family business. I helped my customers select floor and wall coverings, which were some of their final decisions in the course of building or remodeling their homes. One would assume that building a house specifically designed to your needs would be a tremendous blessing. But when you hire a contractor to build your house, each day you are pushed to make dozens of decisions about things you've never given a moment's thought in your entire life. Inside or outside hinges? Solid core or stranded wiring? Copper or PVC pipes? It can become overwhelming.

After a month or so of being inundated with choices, you become stupefied and want someone else to decide for a change. You actually want to give up your power to choose and go back to the simple child-like state of someone else deciding things for you. I saw this scenario played out time after time with my customers.

This morning, I read an article about the gear you need to start biking for exercise. It listed eleven things a potential biker must have, including special shoes, shorts, jersey, glasses, helmet, saddle bags, gloves, water bottle, computer to track your progress, CO_2 tire inflator, and last but not least, a bike. In 1972, what did you need? A bike. Has free enterprise run amuck?

There is a popular movement on the internet that helps people simplify their lives. The goal is to pare down and live with only one hundred possessions.

During our bohemian days in Greece, we wouldn't have tallied up one hundred things if we had combined the paraphernalia of the whole family and counted each sock separately. We led a simple and stress-free life. We really never missed having lots of belongings. We had enough, just enough, and that was fine. Making a house into a home isn't about the objects in it.

Our rustic kitchen was the heart of our home. It had a worn appearance, which cannot be duplicated by decorators, no matter how hard they try to achieve a shabby chic look. I had no complicated gadgets or small appliances in Greece. I did without a blender or mixer. In fact, I didn't even have a whisk.

Contemporary cooks think they can't prepare a proper meal without a pantry full of small appliances and new-fangled tools, but I have proved it can be done. I think the freshness, careful aging, and quality of the food we consumed in Greece trumped the need for special tools. My unsophisticated mixer was an old wooden spoon, and my whisk was a fork.

I had one big skillet with a lid, a stew pot, a large saucepan, and a small saucepan. That was it, and there was no Teflon to be found on any of them. I did most of the food preparation at the kitchen table, because of the lack of counter space.

I hadn't thought to bring any written recipes, so I was cooking from scratch, by memory and spur of the moment invention.

My grandmother taught me the 'art of stirring'. She showed me how to make egg noodles with my bare hands and hang them on the back of the slatted kitchen chairs to dry. She made her own yogurt decades before it became popular to do so. My food philosophy in a nutshell is '*if my grandmother wouldn't recognize something as food, it's probably not good for my family'*. She never saw a juice box or a tube of yogurt. She would wonder what they were. I often think of her when I'm cooking for my family. She's there with me in spirit.

I picked a plum of insight by living so simply. It made me appreciate what I have. It clarified my thinking and made me realize what is really important in life. Nowadays, I can own nearly anything I might want, but I see that lots of things would own me if I had them. I would be their slave.

However, after washing thousands of diapers by hand, I do have a deep appreciation for the hum of a washer and dryer. I would hate to go back to washing everything in the old baby bathtub.

I know women whose only occupation is shopping. No other pastime gives them more pleasure than acquiring something new. They pay more for a handbag than I spend to feed my family for two months. I would never splurge like that, even if I were a millionaire. I like the challenge of living a rich life without spending much money.

Henry David Thoreau said, "Our life is frittered away by detail. Simplify, simplify." I think he was right.

I believe the greatest sense of discontentment and depression comes from the idea that we are lacking something. Buying and having may distract you for a moment, but they won't make you happier.

The families I met in Kato living very simply, all together in one small room, were some of the happiest people I've ever known.

In Greece, I was living what had been the traditional American wife's role since the end of World War II: working inside the home and caring for our children. It was a part I was trained for and expected to play. No one at my high school ever suggested I go to college, even though I was ranked in the top ten percent of my class. At the time, girls went to college only if they planned to be a teacher, a nurse, or didn't want to get married.

Most of us thought getting married and being supported by our husbands was the natural order of things. This scenario was played out for us daily on television shows like *Leave it to Beaver* and *The Donna Reed Show*. Dreams played around my naïve teenage brain when I saw the hope chest ads in *Seventeen Magazine*. The unspoken promise was we would all have loving marriages, orderly homes, and beautiful children.

The women of the 1940s called to work in factories during World War II lost their jobs when Johnny came marching home. Rosie the Riveter returned to her kitchen, and apparently most Americans believed she would never again be called on to support her family.

Betty Friedan had posed the question 'Is that all there is?' in her book *The Feminine Mystique* in 1963. She co-founded the National Organization for Women in 1966. These events had no impact on my life whatsoever.

In 1970, NOW sponsored the Women's Strike for Equality. Taking a page from the Civil Rights Movement, a group of women and a few men marched down Fifth Avenue in New York City carrying signs, singing, and chanting. Speakers Friedan, Gloria Steinem, and Bella Abzug whipped the crowd into a frenzy of excitement. Traffic came to a halt. Americans across the country saw the protest on the evening news, and it got our attention.

Suffragette Alice Paul drafted the Equal Rights Amendment back in 1923. This was three years after the Nineteenth Amendment to the Constitution gave women the right to vote. In 1971, forty-eight years after it was written, the Equal Rights Amendment was finally passed by Congress and sent to the states for ratification. The approval of thirty-eight states was needed in order to amend our Constitution. A deadline was set for June 30, 1982. Thirty states voted to approve in a little more than a year's time. But then a backlash began to emerge. The wheels of equality grind very slowly.

Women, as well as men, fought the amendment. The Stop ERA groundswell brought up the questions of women being drafted into the military, changes in sexual roles, and abortion rights. The drafting of men to fight the Vietnam War had a huge effect on almost every American. Focusing on that issue was a smart strategy on the anti-ERA movement's part.

Some women wanted the right to control their own bodies with access to safe legal abortions, while others believed in the sanctity of all life. This controversy still rages on today. Sexual behavior had changed fast during the Sixties, mainly due to the birth control pill, which frightened many people. They preferred the repressed morals of the Fifties.

In 1973, the Supreme Court struck down the strict abortion laws of many states when they decided the Roe vs. Wade case. That decision rallied the remaining ERA ratification holdouts. Some of the states rescinded their approval of the amendment. The ratification effort ended three states short of the required majority.

All subsequent attempts to revive the Equal Rights Amendment have failed.

In 1972, our family returned to a changing America. Consumers wanted more cars and nicer homes. They really 'needed' all those items they saw on television. Those needs, an energy crisis, and the burden of taxes gradually eased women into the work force. The American way of life has never been the same.

Today, many women are more educated and earn more than their spouses. Thus, the female sex has been empowered like never before in history, even without the Equal Rights Amendment.

In Kato, I was content to be a wife and homemaker. I couldn't have obtained a Greek work visa anyway.

Cue the music:
"Pictures of Matchstick Men"
Status Quo

Inside our home during the heat of the day, the kids and I drew pictures and sang songs. Our untrained voices blended on "Jesus Loves Me", "The Alphabet Song", and "Zip-a-Dee-Doo-Dah". Sometimes we used pans and spoons for musical instruments. Our serene neighbors probably thought we were nuts, but we had fun doing these simple things.

Late afternoon was our quiet time for reading and naps. I would read aloud from our book of classic children's stories or improvise a tale from memory. I always read to Matt and Tammy, no matter how small they were. I think it instilled in them a love of reading and expanded their vocabularies. Our family members are now all voracious readers, and both our children have grown up to be talented writers. Matt writes fiction, and Tammy writes technical articles for medical journals.

"We've just about plowed our way through the det library," Al said late in the summer. "We've read almost every book they have."

"I guess we can read *A Woman of the People* again."

That novel was a page-turner about a young pioneer girl captured by Comanches who grows up in the Indian culture. We both enjoyed reading a story about the American West we had left behind.

Books are as important to me as food. If I had to go a day without reading, it would be a huge sacrifice. I have a Kindle now, with which I can download thousands of volumes, but I still love the feel of a dog- eared classic resting on my midriff as I recline on a comfortable bed at the end of the day.

While the children napped, I would straighten the house and start dinner. Al returned after his twelve- hour shift, and we would all dine together at the kitchen table. I've always tried to have a sit-down meal for the family each day, even when our kids were busy teenagers and I was working. Mealtime is a good opportunity to talk over the events of the day in a tranquil and stable atmosphere. It seems that almost anything can be discussed over dinner.

After cleaning up the dishes, we would sometimes take a walk and talk about our future when we got back to the States. We planned to open a business, and Al was already making arrangements by mail. Having something to look forward to is a basic human need.

When night fell the stars emerged, brilliant against the inky darkness. There were few electric lights to interfere with the natural light show.

Twilight also brought mosquitoes. Our windows had no screens, and the pests would fly in between the slats of our window shutters. Eventually, someone clued us in about mosquito coils. They were spiral-shaped loops of incense about the size of a dinner plate, infused with a repellant of some sort. The coil balanced on a metal holder. We would light the outer edge with a match, and the incense would smolder gradually throughout the night until it was completely burned. The device abated the nightly bloodletting somewhat. We used countless boxes of them throughout the summer, and I learned how much a simple invention like wire window screen can improve your life.

One day that summer, I decided to try the Kato tap water. How bad could it be? Our neighbors seemed to be doing fine drinking it. It would be so much easier to use the tap water instead of hauling water from the det all the time.

I tentatively swished the water around my mouth and spit it out in the sink. I didn't swallow, though it tasted just fine.

A few hours later, I began to feel nauseous. Soon I was bent over vomiting, and I was sick for the following two days. It was a hard lesson learned. When they say, "Don't drink the water," pay attention. At least I had only used myself as a guinea pig and had not dosed the whole family.

One morning Matt got up early before the rest of the household. While we slept, he crept into the kitchen and opened the cupboard where the food was kept. All our storage spaces were low and easily accessible for a hungry toddler. He started grazing on whatever he could find.

Then he worked his way around to the sink and found a box of clothes detergent underneath it. I believe he intended to merely carry it around with him, but apparently he had the box upside down. The soap powder poured out of the spout everywhere he walked.

When I awoke and came into the kitchen, the marble floor was almost completely covered with detergent powder. Matt was trying to clean up the mess with the broom and dustpan. We all had a good laugh, and the kitchen smelled extremely fresh for weeks afterward.

On one of our trips to Athens to the Air Force Base Commissary, I was able to purchase some Rit Dye and some basic white cotton t-shirts. Feeling a creative urge when we got home, we set up the baby bathtub in the back yard and created some fashionable tie-dye shirts. We had red, blue, yellow, and orange dye. All the shirts came out looking like we had a target on our chest, but we wore them proudly. Fortunately, there were no serious mishaps with the dye and the kids.

Looking back at the early Seventies, I realize we were entering the worst fashion decade in American history. Prior to then, few modern men had expressed themselves with faddish attire. Clothing design had been a female interest, except for Elton John and few other nonconformists. But the Seventies man embraced style wholeheartedly.

Men who had no idea what an 'outfit' was were now wearing them. Their hair was longer and fluffier, and they had long muttonchop sideburns. Many had droopy walrus-like mustaches. Their loudly striped shirts were tight and tapered with big floppy collars. Large plaids and bright colored fabrics were made into pants. The pants were tight, too, (or too tight) with bell bottoms. Pants like these had never been seen before or since. On their feet were the ubiquitous Dingo boots.

Female attire had been heavily influenced by the hippie scene, but males didn't seem to like the look unless they were real hippies. It took a while, but Carnaby Street and the British music invasion was what finally brought these fashion wallflowers to the dance.

The airmen of Araxos Detachment had little opportunity to participate in the preening and primping. They had to keep their hair cut 'high and tight', and their mustaches neatly trimmed. Dull green fatigues were the uniform of the day.

A universal truth is that women love shoes. I am no exception. The entire family got new shoes while we lived in Greece. We bought handmade sandals in the Monastiraki section near the Acropolis in Athens. Mine had a leather sole, a loop to go around the big toe, and a leather strap across the top of my foot. They were the simplest of shoes, but really comfortable. My Greek size was a 40, instead of my American size 7. Matt and Tammy got traditional t-strap children's shoes for their growing feet, and Al got Greek fisherman's sandals.

Being a shoe glutton, I also bought two pairs of Italian shoes in Patras. One pair were braided white leather clogs for summer, and the other pair for winter were unusual brown suede flats that wrapped around my ankle. They were decades ahead of their time. Similar designs are shown today on Paris runways.

The Italians sure know their way around the curvature of the human foot. The shoes I bought fit like gloves and required no breaking in period. I wore them for many years back in the States, and they drew many appreciative glances, because they were so unique.

On one occasion, Al and I rented some bicycles and explored the countryside around Kato. We rode past the blood orange groves that surround the village. We had purchased blood oranges at the market in Kato. Today they are a favorite ingredient for gourmands, but in the early 1970s I had never heard of them.

The fruit looked like a standard Florida orange, until it was cut open to reveal the deep scarlet center. The ones we ate were more tart than sweet. Many houses in town had orange, lemon, and limes trees close by. Citrus is a popular flavor in all courses of Greek meals, from soup like *avgolemono* to desserts like *keik siropi lemonati*.

On our bicycle ride, I remember seeing an unusual two-story house with a balcony. A colorful flowering vine clung to the side of the house and the balcony with purple blossoms hanging down like clusters of grapes. What a charming scene it made.

Most homeowners in and around Kato had grapevines growing over pergolas of some type adjacent to their houses. The vines provided food and dappled shade for the occupants. The grapes could be eaten fresh, dried into raisins, or crushed into wine and *tsipouro*. The frugal homeowners even used the grape leaves for *dolmades*, a finger food that sometimes accompanied a salad plate. The neatly-rolled grape leaves held seasoned rice, onions, and pine nuts, and sometimes ground lamb.

Many of the Greek families around us were primarily vegetarian, eating meat only on Sunday. Lots of their recipes had two versions: with or without meat. Fish and squid were eaten more often than meat. Most of the rural people had sheep and goats, but they seldom butchered them. The animals were kept for their wool and their milk, which was made into cheese and yogurt.

During the hottest days of the summer, Kato began experiencing electrical brownouts. We would notice the naked light bulbs in our house gradually becoming dimmer and dimmer. The power never completely failed, but we were worried about our precious refrigerator's motor burning out. When the power came back to full force, it usually surged. The room got much brighter than normal. The electrical infrastructure must not have been able to carry much of a load. No one in Kato had air conditioning, and only a few had refrigerators.

Once, the water pump for the whole village failed, and we were without running water for three days. Of course, we had our five gallon drinking water jug at hand, which Al refilled at the detachment. Our tribe was pretty grungy by the time the water pump was repaired.

Cue the music:
"Your Song"
Elton John

Greek airmen.

Matt and Tammy on our porch.

Me with my gardenia plant.

Matt by the Trion Symmahon Square clock.

A photographer in a square in Patras.

The sheltering Nafpaktos harbor.

Weary travelers on the ferry back from Nafpaktos.

Matt and I cranking the Peanut.

Kato children proudly march with their flag on Greek
Independence Day.

A soccer match in a vacant lot in Kato.

A horse-drawn hearse in Kato.

Al paddling near the Araxos beach.

Feeding Tammy in her playpen at the Araxos beach.

Playing in the surf at Araxos beach.

A Greek woman selling a live pig at the Kato street market.

Holding anise cookies and Easter eggs.

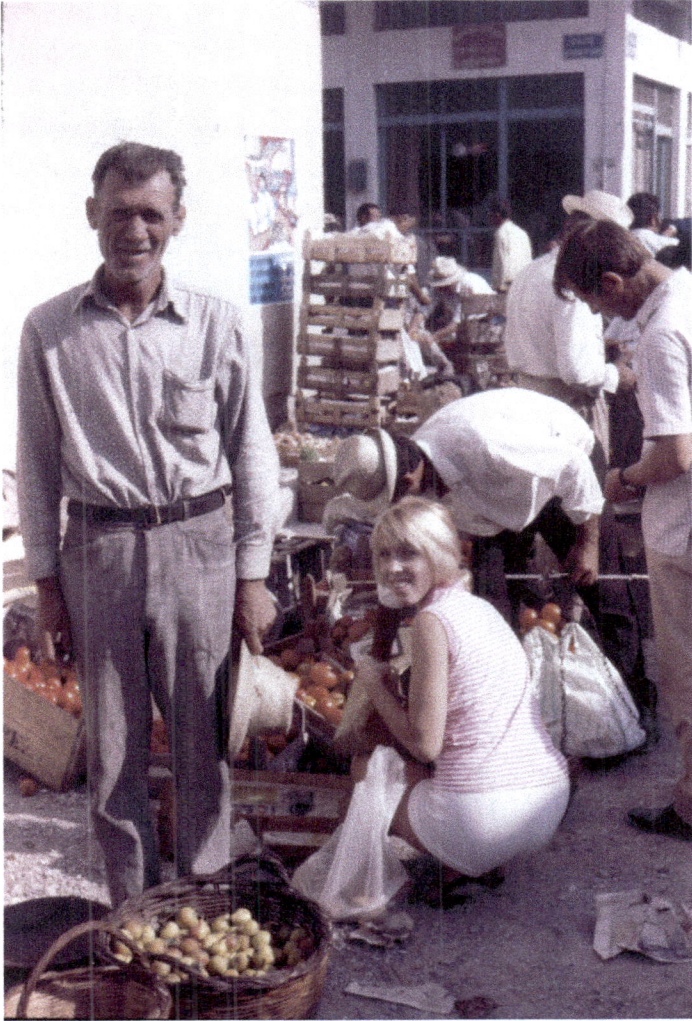

Buying vegetables at the Kato farmers' market.

'Souvlaki Rock', our landmark on the road to Athens.

Shopping with friends in the streets of Athens.

The Corinth Canal.

An archeological dig in the heart of Athens.

Taking in the panoramic view from the Acropolis in Athens.

Al on the steps of the Parthenon in Athens.

Posing with the Caryatids in Athens.

Our family on a bench near the Acropolis.

10 – OVER UNDER SIDEWAYS DOWN

Al spent his long workdays in the corrugated tin-roofed radio shack at the Araxos Detachment. You might wonder why the small group of airmen was sent to such a remote location. Americans were in Greece as a part of the North Atlantic Treaty Organization or NATO. If you or your spouse have been in the military, you know they use acronyms for everything. You have to learn the jargon to keep up with the conversation.

NATO is a military alliance formed in 1949 to collectively defend its members, which were the United States, Canada, Norway, Denmark, Iceland, Italy, and Portugal. The coalition came into being immediately after World War II and before the Korean Conflict began.

The first Secretary General, Lord Hastings 'Pug' Ismay, stated that the goal of NATO was 'to keep the Russians out, the Americans in, and the Germans down'. The member countries agreed that an armed attack against any one of them would be considered an attack against all.

Throughout my entire life, America has been the world's policeman. I have always wondered why. I studied our history and learned that the American people and their leaders thought World War I was 'the war to end all wars'. After that war, America entered a period of isolationism.

Then World War II broke out, and the US was drawn into the battle when bombs rained down on Pearl Harbor. Many citizens and their representatives in Congress concluded, rightly or wrongly, that isolationism was the cause of the Second World War.

Since the end of World War II, America has been hyper-vigilant, ingratiating the US into political systems worldwide.

We have a military presence in over one hundred fifty countries out of one hundred ninety-six existing in the world today. Sleuthing out the exact number of bases around the globe is like nailing Jell-o to the wall. The Pentagon says six hundred sixty-two. Other sources say seven hundred fifty.

The global empires established by Alexander the Great, the Romans, and the British cannot compare to the scope of America's outspread wings of protection. This unwavering watchfulness holds our enemies at arm's length.

The time between World War I and II was short. It has been nearly seven decades since the crew of the Enola Gay dropped the atomic bomb called 'Little Boy' on Hiroshima, resulting in Japanese capitulation. Most observers would conclude we must continue our vigilance. The thought of what World War III might bring is too much to bear for the 'duck and cover' generation. Our teachers made us practice hiding under our desks and covering our heads in case of a nuclear attack. Even as a second-grader, I knew that wouldn't help.

As a child of the Fifties, I grew up praying every night that THE BOMB would not be dropped on America, and that we would all wake up the next morning. Talk of bomb shelters, radioactive fallout, and the imminent threat hanging over us was never far from my mind.

It is normal for a child to be afraid of the dark, of the bogeyman under the bed, or of being separated from their mother and father, but children shouldn't have to fear nuclear weapons.

Today, NATO includes twenty-eight member countries, and twenty-two additional countries participate in the Partnership for Peace. The combined military budget of all NATO members makes up approximately seventy percent of all military spending worldwide.

In 1952, the USA and Britain challenged the inclusion of

Greece and Turkey, because they believed the two countries weren't militarily in the same league as the other members. Greece and Turkey's longstanding inability to get along with each other probably was also on many minds.

Even though we spoke very little Greek, we clearly understood that the Greeks intensely hated the Turks and strongly disliked the Armenians.

The dissenters were overruled. That's why Al was in Greece, sitting by himself and wearing Air Force fatigues in a tin-roofed shed. The American government insisted upon oversight. The Hellenic Air Force Base near Araxos housed nuclear weapons, probably provided by NATO, but I can't say for sure. The American Air Force was nearby at their detachment to assure Washington, DC and the American people that all was well.

Each hour of every day, an all-clear authentication code had to be received and sent like clockwork. Once, before Al arrived at Araxos, another radio man fell asleep on the job. When he didn't received the authentication code and send it on, all hell broke loose. Within minutes, armored vehicles drove into Araxos at full speed, throwing up gravel. They came to an abrupt stop, and several men bailed out. The radio man was rudely awakened. I don't know what consequences he suffered, but the story was used as a cautionary tale to all future radio men.

The coalition of NATO members brought about a standardization of military practices and procedures among the members. Basically, all the other countries adopted the United States' way of operating. The NATO Phonetic Alphabet became the standard worldwide, allowing critical radio voice messages to be clearly understood, regardless of the operator's accent, be they Turkish or Texan. The Federal Aviation Administration and the American Radio Relay League also use the alphabet.

Al could have been sent to a much more dangerous post

than Araxos. The year before we went to Greece, he heard a warning through the military grapevine to expect deployment to an outpost along the Vietnam-Laos border. The radio relay shacks there were on mountain tops. He heard rumors that no radio operator had survived and come back home from the remote post.

When I heard that, my family preservation instincts went into overdrive. I suspected I might be about two weeks pregnant. It was too early to be allowed to see my usual military doctor, so I went to a civilian clinic to have a pregnancy test. The results were positive, and Al received a deferral from the perilous deployment. We stayed in Colorado Springs until he received his orders for Araxos. Babies are blessings, but our daughter was a double blessing for us.

Twice while we lived in Greece, Al was allowed to use the radio to contact ham radio operators who belonged to the Radio Relay League in the southern United States. The hams called Al's parents' home telephone collect, and then Al was able to talk to his folks over his radio.

After he spoke, he would say, "Over," and then his mom and dad would speak and do the same. Al's dad really got a kick out of that. He hadn't used radio lingo since he was an Army Air Corp bomber during World War II.

Calling home in 1972 was a far cry from today, when soldiers on the front lines can use a cell phone or email their family back home. They can even see each other using Skype. I didn't get to talk by telephone to my family for the entire year. Our letters were our link to the people back home.

Forty years after Al's stint at Araxos, he can still recite the phonetic alphabet he used there, forward and backward.

Letter:	Code Word:	Pronunciation:
A	Alpha	Al fah
B	Bravo	Brah Voh
C	Charlie	Char Lee
D	Delta	Dell Tah
E	Echo	Eck Oh
F	Foxtrot	Foks Trot
G	Golf	Golf
H	Hotel	Hoh Tell (FAA, IMO, ITU) Ho Tell (ICAO)
I	India	In Dee Ah
J	Juliett	Jew Lee Ett
K	Kilo	Key Loh
L	Lima	Lee Mah
M	Mike	Mike
N	November	No Vem Ber
O	Oscar	Oss Car
P	Papa	Pah Pah
Q	Quebec	Keh Beck
R	Romeo	Row Me Oh
S	Sierra	See Air Ah (FAA) See Air Rah (ICAO, IMO, ITU)
T	Tango	Tang Go
U	Uniform	You Nee Form
V	Victor	Vik Tah
W	Whiskey	Wiss Key
X	X Ray	Ecks Ray
Y	Yankee	Yang Key
Z	Zulu	Zoo Loo

Certain phonetic letters came to be short versions of phrases. Bravo Zulu means 'well done'. Zulu time stands for 'Greenwich Mean Time', and the American nickname for the Viet Cong, 'Charlie', comes from Victor Charlie. Victor Charlie was shortened to VC and then to simply Charlie.

Cue the music:
"For What It's Worth"
Buffalo Springfield

While we were living in Greece, there was a climate of discontent and rebellion back home. On January 4, 1971, President Richard Nixon said, "The end is in sight," referring to the Vietnam War. Seven hundred thousand young men had been drafted into military service, with the average age of twenty-three. The reality of the draft affected every community. We all had friends and neighbors fighting in the jungles of Southeast Asia. It was a different kind of war than our country had fought before.

Vietnam was the first war to take place in American living rooms via the televised nightly news. American universities were bulging at their seams with young men avoiding the draft by education deferrals. If grades slipped, they would be drafted right away.

Many Americans were convinced the war was morally wrong. Twelve thousand people were arrested in early May, 1971, for demonstrating in Washington, DC. Mass protests, sit-ins, and love-ins sprang up all over the country. Our soldiers began leaving Vietnam in 1971.

On July 18, 1972, actress Jane Fonda visited Vietnam and broadcast her anti-war message over Hanoi radio, an act many Americans have yet to forgive her for. She was photographed sitting on a North Vietnamese anti-aircraft gun, which may have been used against our own troops. In 1971, she earned the Academy Award for Best Actress. In 1972, she earned the nickname 'Hanoi Jane'.

On August 23, 1972, the last combat troops departed Vietnam. Two years and eight months after that, the last American civilians left the country. Two hours later, the Viet

Cong flag was raised over the presidential palace. Don't let the screen door hit you on the way out.

In total, 58,269 American soldiers were killed in action and 303,704 were wounded with approximately half that requiring hospitalization.

Many Americans back in the States mistakenly blamed all US soldiers for the misguided war, when they should have blamed the old men with the power to end it. Returning soldiers were not given parades and thanked for their service. Instead they received hatred and verbal abuse. Some were called 'baby killer'. Even military personnel who weren't anywhere near Vietnam were included in the mass disdain.

The Vietnam draft enlightened America's young people to the fact that not everyone is equal in the USA, despite what we had been taught our whole lives. Some are more equal than others.

Sons of the rich and powerful managed to escape being drafted. If you knew the right people and pulled the right strings, you could avoid the inconvenient interruption of your perfect life.

Cue the music:
"On the Road Again"
Canned Heat

This is an excerpt from young Bill Clinton's letter to Colonel Eugene Holmes, who had himself survived the Bataan Death March and being held captive as a POW during World War II:

"First, I want to thank you, not only for saving me from the draft, but for being so kind to me last summer, when I was as low as I have ever been."

Clinton wasn't rich or powerful at that time, but he was working on it. Being a Rhodes Scholar at Oxford allowed him to network with some highly influential people, who in turn knew other powerful individuals. He preferred Oxford, England, over Canada, where most of the draft dodgers ended up.

America lost its innocence during this period, and it would never again blindly believe what it was told.

Cue the music:
"Fortunate Son"
Creedence Clearwater Revival

Last Saturday, the citizens of Victoria, Texas, where I live now, gathered around the town square at ten o'clock in the morning. 'The Parade That Never Was' started promptly and gave closure to hundreds of Vietnam vets and the people who called them their heroes.

For close to two hours, groups and marching bands honored the men and women who gave selflessly to serve their country in Vietnam. Then, trailer after trailer rolled down the parade route, carrying hundreds of surviving veterans. Three veteran brothers from one family were there. The county's most decorated veteran marched proudly down the center of the street, his chest covered with medals and ribbons.

The vets are older now, and some aren't doing too well. Even though they are not as strong as they once were, they hold themselves with quiet dignity.

The crowd cheered, held signs, and waved Old Glory. I caught the eyes of several vets, holding my sign that read, 'Thank you for your sacrifice'. I thought about other slogans, but then I remembered how many people I knew gave the first four or five years of their adult lives to Vietnam. They might have been starting their families, buying homes, and building their careers. Instead, they went thousands of miles from home to an unforgiving jungle to preserve the American way of life. I finally got to thank them.

Cue the music:
"Heart Full of Soul"
The Yardbirds

How does a leader who starts out with the best intentions suddenly veer off course and plow the ship of state right into an iceberg? Richard Nixon began as a statesman, but ended up as a man with feet of clay.

He portrayed himself as rock solid at a time when Americans craved stability. The assassinations of John F. Kennedy, Martin Luther King Jr., and Bobby Kennedy, along with the ongoing political unrest made many citizens feel their country was crumbling.

When we left America for Greece in 1971, Nixon was president, and he was Al's commander in chief. US forces were gradually leaving Vietnam. Nixon was credited or blamed, depending on your viewpoint, for starting the War on Drugs, the Environmental Protection Agency, and enforcing desegregation in the South.

John Dalberg-Acton said, "Power tends to corrupt, and absolute power corrupts absolutely." He learned that from history, but he could have been talking about the Nixon administration.

Nixon once aspired to join the FBI. He was hired, but never started, due to budget cuts. His first calling exposes his natural bent for undercover power broking and dirty tricks.

On June 17, 1972, five White House burglars were caught breaking into the Democratic Party Headquarters at the Watergate Complex in Washington, DC. They planned to 'bug' the offices with listening devices in order to spy on their political opponents.

On October 10, the *Washington Post* published a story by reporters Carl Bernstein and Bob Woodward:

"FBI agents have established that the Watergate bugging incident stemmed from a massive campaign of political spying and sabotage conducted on behalf of President Nixon's re-election and directed by officials of the White House and the Committee for the Reelection of the President."

As we neared the fortieth anniversary of the break-in, Woodward and Bernstein said the corruption was even worse than what they exposed back in 1972.

Now that all the evidence has been examined and the transcripts have been studied at length, it is evident that Nixon ordered harassment of anti-war activists and his political opponents by the FBI, the CIA, and the IRS. He would stop at nothing to sabotage his enemies.

Nixon managed to distance himself from the Watergate scandal. Less than a month after the *Post* story broke, he won re-election over George McGovern by a landslide. I think voters of that time could not conceive that the highest office holder in the land could stoop so low.

But Nixon's Achilles heel turned out to be his penchant for taping conversations in the Oval Office. When a White House aide testified that Nixon had a secret recording device, the tapes were subpoenaed. His house of cards began to fall. Nixon was caught on tape talking about using the CIA to obstruct the FBI. When the taped conversations were revealed, he lost support even from his own party. On November 17, 1973, he gave his famous 'I am not a crook' speech.

Facing impeachment, Nixon chose to resign on August 9, 1974. In his resignation speech from the Oval Office, he devoted half the oration to his accomplishments as president. He never admitted any guilt. He smiled broadly and gave the 'V for victory' sign with both hands as he boarded the helicopter to leave the White House for the last time.

Nixon's successor, Gerald Ford, granted Nixon a full pardon, which barred any future indictment. The pardon outraged many Americans. They gave Nixon the nickname 'Tricky Dick'.

Nixon lived a quiet life out of the public eye for the next twenty years until he suffered a stroke and died April 22, 1994.

The wise ancient Greek philosopher Socrates said, "I was too honest a man to be a politician and live."

Socrates believed in fairness and the rights of all people, be they prince or pauper. The Socratic philosophy is the basis for many of our fundamental American beliefs. He stepped on too many Athenian toes. For that sin, he was executed by being forced to swallow poison hemlock.

Cue the music:
"Heart of Gold"
Neil Young

The violence of the 1960s and early 1970s spawned the hippie counter culture. The Vietnam War, multiple assassinations, corruption at the highest level, and riots shook the country to its core. Americans longed for assurance that the country's backbone was still strong and our values were rock solid.

Hippies espoused love, peace, communal living, unique ways of dressing, long hair and beards, the sexual revolution, and drugs. They opposed traditional ways of life, to which they attributed the war and all of the ills of American society.

Hippie subculture can be traced all the way back to ancient Greece. Diogenes the Cynic lived around 350 BC and was recorded history's first hippie. He was a beggar, sleeping in a barrel turned on its side on the street.

All his energy was devoted to debunking traditional ways of living. He sometimes carried a lamp around town during the daytime, saying he was looking for an honest man. He claimed he never found one.

The hippies of the 1960s loved camping, hiking, informal socializing, and spontaneous music. Cleanliness was low on their list of priorities. The movement was a stark contrast to the straight arrow 1950s when men wore suits and ties, women wore dresses with hats and gloves, and cleanliness was next to Godliness.

Human beings are defined by the decade into which they are born. Each generation mourns for the next generation. We are sure the youngsters are missing out on all the wonders of the childhood we had.

Universally, each new batch of offspring, as they come into their own, believes they have invented sex. Every generation thinks theirs is 'the greatest generation'.

People especially idealize the decade of their teenage years. Our first taste of freedom and individualism, while still being protected and nurtured by good old mom and dad, is the most marvelous time of our lives. We desire the world to be forever like it was when we were teens. Grown-ups wear the image of that decade like a brand.

Most cultural movements start with high ideals, but because human beings are involved, usually these visions of utopia deteriorate. Such was the hippie culture of the Sixties. Bending long-held sexual mores can make life get conspicuously messy, and undisciplined drug use can have unintended consequences. The Manson 'family' is a prime example.

Right before Easter in 1966, *Time Magazine* posed the question, 'Is God Dead?' in bright red letters on a black background on its cover. The article inside questioned whether God was being pushed out of modern America.

The question struck a nerve and started a huge controversy. Thousands of people took time to write letters to the editor of *Time*. Everyone I knew was talking about it, and we discussed it in our classrooms at length.

The hippie movement hatched another subculture within its ranks, which had lasting positive effects. During the late 1960s and early 1970s, the grass roots Jesus movement sprang up in the USA and eventually spread to Europe.

The name 'Jesus Freak' was originally intended as a demeaning moniker, but that was turned around when the movement embraced the name. The Freaks rejected the negative aspects of the hippie lifestyle and adopted the ideas of simple living, belief in miracles, signs, prayer, and universal love.

Some of the Jesus Freaks lived communally. The most visible groups were the well-organized Children of God and the Campus Crusade for Christ.

The pinnacle of the movement was a gathering in Dallas in 1972, which has been called the Christian Woodstock. Between eighty and one hundred thousand young people showed up at the Cotton Bowl. Many of the attendees were traditional church members.

Over five days, the Freaks and the traditionalists mingled while listening to Billy Graham speak, and many stellar musical acts performed. Johnny Cash and Kris Kristofferson were among the performers. The traditionalists took the new music vibe back to their churches, and the current contemporary Christian music genre was born.

Rock and heavy metal music had never before been associated with anything but sex, drugs, and escapism. But even the wildest of rock and roll gods seem to settle into domesticity eventually. Keith Richards talks about driving his kids to school.

The roosters of rock do, however, seem to pair up most often with supermodels.

Today our casual way of dressing and even the popularity of yogurt can be attributed to the hippie movement.

Cue the music:
"More Love"
Smokey Robinson and the Miracles

11 – Hot Fun in the Summertime

I was born a water baby. My parents say I arrived in the world knowing how to swim. At age five, I learned to water ski standing on the front of my dad's skis.

Then he built me a pair of my own, and off I went. Knowing this about me, you might perceive how much I anticipated dipping my toes into the Mediterranean.

All through the wintery wet season, the ultramarine waters waited for me. They were there beckoning each time we drove to Athens, Patras, or to the Araxos Detachment. The sparkling sea showed me every shade of blue, from the lightest azure to the darkest sapphire.

A few preemptory attempts made me realize merely living in Greece hadn't made me a Spartan. The water was icy. I would have to wait for genuine hot weather. Then my sun-warmed skin could overcome the shocking cold.

Throughout recorded history, people have shunned a tan complexion. Ancient Romans used white lead powder to lighten their skin, which resulted in the inevitable permanent pallor of death.

Elizabethans apparently learned nothing from history. They also used lead powder liberally over their faces, shoulders, and bosoms with the same results. Women even went so far as having themselves bled to enhance their ivory appearance.

This all changed in the 1920s when trendsetter, Coco Chanel, went away on holiday, forgot her hat, and returned suntanned. On her, it looked pretty good. About that time Josephine Baker, a coffee-colored goddess, hit Paris hard. Suddenly, tan skin was the toast of the town.

The trend continued to build after World War II. Returning

American GIs used the skills they learned while defending our country to fuel a boat building and water sport craze. The bikini was invented, and it received lots of attention worldwide.

Beautiful tropical Hawaii became the fiftieth state in the Union. For the first time in mankind's long saga, a suntan was seen as a sign of status and wealth.

Madison Avenue advertising executives picked up on the trend and ran with it. All baby boomers know the fragrance of baby oil and cocoa butter, because we spent every summer of the entire decade of the Sixties slathered with the stuff, lying by a pool or on a beach with a transistor radio stuck to the side of our head.

The singers on those radios weren't much older than us. They expressed the plaintive mating call of the American teenager . . . 'Be my Little Baby, but Will You Love Me Tomorrow?'

It was all about the sun, our friends, and the music. Beach songs and beach movies fueled the fire. Teenage girls all wanted to be Gidget, and the boys wanted to be Moondoggie. Surfers were no longer bums. They were considered vibrant, healthy people living life to its fullest.

As soon as the days reached eighty degrees in Kato, the Americans moved their meeting place from the mess hall patio to the American beach. I don't know why the higher-ups at Araxos decided we should have our own private beach, but they were probably wise. Boisterous Americans in skimpy bathing suits would have irritated the local fishing community.

One airman even managed to bring his fancy fiberglass ski boat with a loud outboard motor there. I don't know what strings he pulled to arrange that. I learned a rather painful lesson about how much more difficult water skiing is in the surf than on a mirror-smooth lake.

There was a little walk-up stand on our beach where we

could order food at the window. Someone usually had something cooking on the grill, too. We spent many happy hours there letting the waves wash over us.

"Hey, Gidget. You sure are getting tan," said our friend John, the smart aleck.

"Better than pale and pasty," I sassed back at him.

The beach was covered with egg-shaped rocks instead of sand. Our daughter, Tammy, wearing her tiny red, white, and blue swim suit, kept trying to pop them into her mouth. We solved the 'don't rock the baby' problem by spreading a blanket over the rocks and placing a wood play pen without a floor in it over the blanket. We had to make sure her little arm couldn't snake out between the bars past the edge of the blanket. The family usually spent three days at the beach each week. We all became tawny with gold streaks in our hair.

We had masks, swim fins, and snorkels, which I put to spectacular use. Swimming in briny sea water makes every fiber of my being feel alive. The Ionian Sea was crystal clear, so the smallest object could be spotted fifteen to twenty feet down. I loved to explore the deep, although the chilly water didn't put on the show one would see in a warm ocean with a coral reef. It was more about seeing one ray gliding effortlessly by in a huge expanse of clear water . . . just me and the ray.

"You goin' in again?" asked Roberta when she saw me backing awkwardly toward the water in mask and flippers. "What do you do down there?"

The other Americans seldom left the beach. They thought it odd I loved to swim so much.

"Oh, I just explore the deep. I could stay down there forever," I said.

One of the things I love most about the underwater world is the quietness. Silence of that magnitude is hard to find above the surface. It tranquilizes me. The power of the waves, currents, and tides fascinates me. The myriad creatures living together, hiding from one while hunting another, intrigue me. The colors produced by broken pieces of sunlight prisming down through the currents delight me.

Oceans and seas cover over seventy percent of the earth. Scientists say they know more about the surface of the moon than they know of the mysterious depths of our blue planet.

Cue the music:
"My Blue Heaven"
Fats Antoine Domino

The ancient Greek culture was at least a thousand years ahead of any other ethnic group when it came to bathing and the health aspects of cleanliness. Bathing in the sea, in a river, or in a spring is depicted hundreds of times in ancient Greek art and the writings of Homer and Plutarch, among others.

A Greek goblet on display at the British Museum depicts sea goddess, Thetis, swimming near the beach with dolphins gamboling around her. It is surprising that most of the indoor showers and baths shown in the archaic art look like they belong in a modern American home or gymnasium.

Archeologists uncovering the 1500 BC Minoan Palace in Crete, the largest of the Greek isles, found elaborate drains and water mains, which showed how important hygienic bathing was to them. Bathtubs were offered to guests first thing upon their arrival, and then dining followed. A hand maiden's job was washing the guest's feet or fully bathing the guests. Kitchen servants practiced hand washing before they served food.

The ancient Greeks thought ignorance equaled not being able to read, write, or swim. Physicians and philosophers touted bathing as giving strength and good health. Healing temples called *asclepeion* were located throughout ancient Greece in proximity to the sea, a river, or a natural spring. One *asclepeion* had both hot and cold running springs for the ultimate spa experience.

An *asclepeion* was located near a spring on the southern slope of the Acropolis in Athens. *Asclepeion* guests would sleep the first night there, and the next morning would report their dreams to the priest. He would prescribe healing rituals, including bathing and restricted dining. Mineral water was consumed for cleanliness inside and out. History records that surgeries were performed while patients slept under the influence of opiates.

Hippocrates, the father of medicine, received his training at an *asclepeion*. His Hippocratic Oath is still used as a standard of conduct for doctors today.

Galen of Pergamon, who is recognized as the ancient world's greatest surgeon, performed intricate eye and brain surgeries around 170 AD that were not attempted again for nearly two thousand years. Dissection of human cadavers was forbidden by the Roman Empire, so the surgeon used animals upon which to practice. From them, he learned and speculated how the human body worked. The ancient Greek physicians practiced cleanliness in a controlled environment, not unlike a modern hospital.

Even the conquering Romans prospered from the knowledge they gained from the Greeks. But, after six hundred years, the Roman Empire came crashing down, and the hellish period known as the Dark Ages began. It was as if all the learning and accomplishments of the Greeks had been lost at sea.

The Palace of Versailles outside Paris is a perfect example of how far society plummeted during the Dark Ages. King Louis XIV created the most audacious home, filled with Baroque furniture and surrounded with intricately designed gardens for himself and his royal family. The place had hundreds of rooms, but no functioning toilets until 1768.

Even then, there were only nine to accommodate the royals. Guests invited to gala balls were forced to defecate in stairwells. The palace was known for its constant stench. Chamber pots were banned, but despite that, they were used and emptied frequently out the nearest window. The period of the Dark Ages brought the dreaded Black Death, the bubonic plague, which devastated the European population. The whole continent was drowning in its own poo and needed a thorough scrubbing.

Thankfully, cultural, intellectual, and artistic ideas began to flower and produced the Renaissance. Otherwise, we would all still be using the thunder bowl.

Even though the Greeks invented indoor plumbing, I still found some *toualletas* there in 1972 that fit right into the Dark Ages. The bus station in Patras had a unisex necessary room. I went in and looked around. There were no fixtures. No shiny white thrones. Just a hole in the center of the floor.

Peering down, I could see water running inside the hole. A mental light bulb went on, and I figured out what the hole was for. The GIs called this type of bathroom a 'bomb site'. You had to hope the previous occupant had good aim.

Another interesting pit stop was the café and bus station at Corinth. The restroom was large and filled with stalls, which were open at the top and bottom. Upon closer inspection, I found each stall door marked with a universal man or woman symbol. The men's and women's stalls were interspersed, all in the same room. Needless to say, I did my business and got out quick. I preferred the bomb site bathroom to the possibility of prying eyes peeking over the stall.

Well now, after all that disturbing imagery, how about a cleansing dip in the briny blue?

Cue the music:
"All Summer Long"
The Beach Boys

As the summer heated up, we Americans began noticing more Europeans flooding into the Peloponnese. Al and I picked up a couple hitchhiking near Patras. They were Vim and Nekki from Holland. We brought them to Kato. They had hitchhiked that far and were tired from traveling. Since no hotel existed, we invited them to stay the night at our house.

We had a delightful time dining together and trying to converse. Later, we received a postcard from them thanking us for our hospitality.

Hitchhiking was common in 1972. We lived in a more innocent and friendly time, before urban legends spread bloodcurdling tales of mayhem on the highway.

Al and I even tried hitching a ride to Patras once for the fun of it. A nicely-groomed Greek man driving a mid-sized sedan picked us up. Luckily, we had not used the forbidden thumbs-up hitchhiking sign, which would have insulted the driver. He dropped us off at the Trion Square, and we thanked him profusely in Greek. We didn't mention we had our own car back at the house. At the end of the day, we rode the bus back to Kato.

About fifteen miles from Kato in the opposite direction from Patras was a radiant stretch of white sand call Kalogria Beach. Using my rudimentary knowledge of Greek, *kalo* means 'good' and *gria* means 'old woman', so I believe Kalogria means 'good old woman'.

A nice hotel, restaurant, and outdoor nightclub with live music were nearby. Once the Americans discovered the Kalogria Beach Hotel, it became a frequent destination. It was a quiet getaway for a family picnic and swimming. Secluded coves offered private beaches. But that soon changed.

When the tourist season picked up, hundreds of Europeans, particularly Yugoslavians, funneled into Kalogria. Yugoslavia is now known as Serbo-Croatia and is northwest of Greece. The 'Yugos' came by every conceivable means of transport, including hitchhiking. A more fun-loving group of people would be hard to find. They enlivened the night life and came up with endless ways to entertain everyone. A beach, which until then had been host to a couple of picnickers and a herd of goats, suddenly looked like South Padre Island during Spring Break.

A newly-arrived American couple from California went to party at Kalogria almost every night that summer. Most of the American wives kept a low profile, but this striking new wife made her presence known to everyone. She was tall and had a straight black ponytail down to her waist. Quiet and retiring, she was not. We heard rumors about drugs being used and abused. The running joke was that her husband's primary job was holding back her ponytail while she was hugging the porcelain wishing well.

It was all fun and games until late one night toward the season's end. On the way home from a night out, the airman drove their Volkswagen Beetle off a narrow bridge. The couple survived, but both had serious facial scars from the accident. A skilled plastic surgeon might have been able to repair the damage left by their injuries, but none was available in our remote location.

Writer Nikos Kazantzakis is believed to have been living in the Kalogria area in 1917 when he met Georgios Zorbas, the engineer of a coal mining business. Georgios exuberantly danced his way into our hearts in Kazantzakis' book *Zorba the Greek* and later in the movie of the same name, starring Anthony Quinn. Taking creative license, Kazantzakis changed the book's setting to Crete and Zorba's first name to Alexis. When asked about his life at Kalogria, Kazantzakis replied that it was all described in his book. Which proves you never know where or when you will meet the most interesting character of your life.

During the summer of 1972, one of the American military wives got hold of a Greek knitting and crochet pattern book. The styles pictured were undeniably chic. They were nothing like the homemade hippie, crappy crafts we had seen back in the States. We all got excited about having something made and found a local Kato woman who would create the items for us for a reasonable fee.

I picked the most outrageous pattern, a crocheted bikini. I got lilac-colored cotton thread and lining material in Patras. I had one fitting, and before long the talented crafter had finished the design. I took the bikini home and sewed the lining in by hand with a needle and thread. It took me quite a bit of nerve to wear it to the beach the first time. After all, I wasn't one of those girls who never get wet. I really swim. But the suit held up beautifully to sand and surf. I still have it in a trunk somewhere.

Cue the music:
"Let's Live for Today"
The Grass Roots

We planned another day trip. This time, the couple who went to the winery with us, an airman, and our family would travel to Nafpaktos. We bought tickets for the roll-on/roll-off ferry boat leaving from Patras harbor. We left our car in Patras and walked onto the ferry.

Nafpaktos is about 15 kilometers across the narrows of the Gulf of Corinth northeast of Patras, as the seagull flies. It was a magnificent day, one of a long string of perfect days of sunny weather.

As the ferry moved out of the harbor, the pungent smell of

motor fuel mixed with the salty air wafted up to us. It reminded me of my childhood summers spent on sandy islands at the lake. We sat on the upper deck, soaking in the sights and sounds, feeling fully alive. Glints of sunlight sparkling across the water made me squint. I dug around in my crocheted bag for my fashionable sunglasses. The huge lenses covered half my face.

Before long, the Nafpaktos port came into view. The sheltering harbor reached out like two Herculean arms with a round turret at each hand. The harbor walls and turrets were made of stacked stone and were crowned with the saw-toothed crenellated edge like we had seen on the battlements at the winery. The gaps in the walls had once contained several cannons, but they were no longer present the day we visited there.

The opening between the turrets wasn't large enough to accommodate many of the vessels of today, but it worked well for centuries as a haven to small watercraft.

"This port looks medieval," Al said.

"I'd guess it's from the same era as the Patras Castle from the way it looks," said Mac.

The well-kept houses encircling the harbor were mostly white stucco with ruddy orange tile roofs. The contrast of the rust-colored roofs against the turquoise water delighted our eyes. The elevation rose sharply behind the village, and we looked up to see the Nafpaktos Fortress. The village of Nafpaktos was formerly known as Lepanto.

We heard the ferry engine throttle back, and the careful maneuvers of docking began. Anticipation welled up in us. Soon the gangplank was lowered, and we disembarked.

Our family and friends meandered down the waterfront. We found an outdoor café nearby and dined on salads, bread, and delicious fresh seafood. Renewed, our group set out to hike up to the fortress. The trail was a gently sloping incline, which hair pinned gradually back and forth. We were shaded by trees, which made for an agreeable walk.

The vantage point at the top of the hill is believed to have belonged to an ancient Greek tribe, the Locrians. The Athenians and the Aetolians controlled it later, until the Romans took possession in 191 BC. It was flourishing until 551 AD when an earthquake, the same one that destroyed the Patras Castle, demolished it. The structure was rebuilt and knocked down at least two more times by earthquakes.

In 1407, the site was purchased by the Venetians, who fortified it so strongly that it successfully defended a four-month-long siege by the thirty thousand man Turkish Army. The fort must have been much more difficult to approach then than it was the day we strolled leisurely up the hill.

The Venetians had a thousand-year-long presence in Greece. They had no large army, but they did have a mighty and effective fleet. Their strategy was to build fortifications that could be defended until assistance arrived by water. The Venetians maintained forty-six forts with walled cities and several more fortified villages in Greece.

The water off the Nafpaktos harbor was the site of a great oar-driven naval struggle, the Battle of Lepanto, in 1571. A large Christian fleet, assembled by Pope Pius V, defeated the Ottoman fleet at great loss of life to both navies.

Galleys of slaves, many of whom were captured Christians, rowed the Ottoman fleet. The skirmish lasted five hours and finished with hand-to-hand sword fighting. The Battle of Lepanto has inspired many works of art, some of which hang in the Doge Palace of Venice, the Prado, and the Spanish Senate Building in Madrid. Pope Pius V was so elated by the Christian triumph, he commissioned Giorgio Vasari to create painted frescoes of the warfare in the Vatican.

Many historians believe the Christian victory was a turning point in human history. The Ottomans lost approximately 30,000 experienced sailors and were forced to release about 12,000 Christian galley slaves. The defeat squelched further Turkish incursions into Europe, saving Italy from invasion.

The renowned Spanish writer, Miguel de Cervantes, participated in the battle aboard the Marquesa, a galley ship of the Holy League Christian fleet. Though taken ill, Cervantes refused to stay below deck. He fought valiantly, saying he would rather die for God and his king than take cover below. Cervantes received two gunshots wounds to the chest and one to his left arm, which rendered the limb useless for the rest of his life. He was hospitalized for six months following the battle.

Many exploits followed, including Cervantes being held as a slave in Algiers for five years. All his adventures were fodder for his writing. In 1605, his masterpiece *Don Quixote* was an immediate success and established him as a literary giant.

The citizens of Nafpaktos have honored Cervantes with a statue and marker near the harbor. Plaques on the harbor wall from the Venetians and the Spanish also commemorate the battle. By treaty in 1832, the fortification became a part of Greece once more after Greek independence was declared.

We climbed around and through the citadel, taking in the expansive views from every vista.

"Look, Al. I can see the Peloponnese across the water," I said, pointing toward the Gulf.

He scanned the horizon. "We're probably looking right at the spot where we had our picnic at the winery."

"It's likely there's someone sitting there right now looking back at us," I observed.

The walls of the fort were generally well maintained and intact. There were arched doorways, steps, and what looked like a cistern for water storage. During the Venetian era, the fortification included two walls that extended from the hilltop fort down to the sea, cradling and protecting the village and harbor. Three other protective walls running parallel to the coastline were at various levels on the hillside.

Late in the afternoon, our little band trudged back down to the harbor and boarded the ferry back to Patras. We were a much quieter group on the way home. Some even stretched out and caught a quick nap, rocked gently by the motion of the boat.

"This is the only way to travel," Al said. "All stretched out in the sun with someone else doing the driving."

"I bet the locals don't agree. I bet it's a real pain to them," our friend Mac added.

The locals probably did get tired of the ferry being the only way to get from the mainland to the Peloponnese. They were forced to use the ferry as their mode of transportation for thirty-two more years until 2004, when the magnificent Charilaos Trikoupis Bridge opened. It is commonly known as the Rio-Antirrio Bridge, because it connects those two cities at the narrowest point of the Gulf of Corinth. Rio is a short distance east of Patras, and Antirrio is west of Nafpaktos.

The span was named for Charilaos Trikoupis, who served seven terms as Prime Minister of Greece between 1875 and 1895. He was the first person to suggest linking the mainland to the Peloponnese with a bridge.

About one hundred years later, planning began. The result was an aesthetic and engineering masterpiece. The bridge is truly a work of art. At 9,449 feet long, it is one of the world's longest multi-span cabled bridges.

Special construction methods were used to allow the piers to move laterally on the seabed in the event of an earthquake. Greece experiences more seismic activity than any other country in Europe. The bridge parts don't have rigid connections, but use jacks and dampers to absorb movement.

The bridge opened just before the 2004 Athens Summer Olympics, and the Olympic torchbearers were the first ones to cross the span. Today, a driver pays a Euro toll equivalent to sixteen American dollars to cross in a car. Larger vehicles pay more.

About five months after the inauguration of the long awaited bridge, one of the cables snapped from the top and crashed down. The bridge was immediately closed. Engineers found that lightning had started a small fire, which had caused the cable to fail. Repairs were made and the bridge was reopened.

Cue the music:
"If You Could Read My Mind"
Gordon Lightfoot

12 – What Is and What Should Never Be

The nights in the countryside around Kato were pitch dark. The stars sparkled above, but it was as if a heavy canvas tarp had been thrown over the entire landscape. Driving to the Araxos Detachment at night on the narrow serpentine road could be perilous. No street lights illuminated the roadway. Add to this the Greek Orthodox priests' habit of wearing long black robes and walking almost everywhere they went. You wind up with a perfect recipe for disaster.

One day late in the summer, Al came home from work and said there had been an accident the night before. An American airman, driving to his mid-shift job a little before eleven, had struck and killed a priest who was walking along the dark highway. The driver was a friend of ours, a family man with a wife and two small children. Their family mirrored ours, and they were from the same area back in the States.

The priest had been on his way to the small fishing village, Niforeika, not far from Kato. Our friend had been handcuffed and taken to jail in Patras, where he remained.

In 1972, crime in Greece was almost non-existent. We Americans were surprised by this, having grown up in the Wild West where crimes from petty theft to murder were banner headlines in the newspaper daily. We wondered how the Greek government had achieved such integrity and uprightness among its citizens.

We heard rumors that all criminals there were punished harshly. Prison stays of undetermined length were meted out for all offenders. Knowing this, we were especially fearful about what would happen to our friend. We felt powerless to help him. We heard through the grapevine that legal counsel was on its way from the Air Force Base in Athens. We prayed that was true.

We knew the driver to be a trustworthy guy who didn't drink and drive. We also knew that if the accident had happened back in the USA, he probably wouldn't have even gotten a ticket. Vehicular manslaughter would only be charged if the driver had shown negligence by speeding, driving recklessly, or driving under the influence of drugs or alcohol, resulting in the death of another person.

But killing an Orthodox priest in Greece was tantamount to killing a police officer in the United States. It was considered a serious crime that couldn't go unpunished.

Weeks passed. We kept hoping our friend would show up in Kato, but he didn't. His wife was worried sick and becoming thinner and thinner each day.

When an American is on foreign soil, an event like this makes you suddenly realize how vulnerable you are. You're not in the land of the free and the home of the brave any longer. They don't do things the American way. You have left your rights back in Oklahoma. Get ready to hear a discouraging word, because you're not home on the range anymore. I began to feel an aching need to go back to my own country, my birthplace, and my family.

When the end of our tour came, our friend was still in jail. We returned to our life in the United States and heard no more about him.

Several years later in 1979, he and his wife showed up unexpectedly at our front door one afternoon. We had a good visit. He didn't want to talk about his imprisonment. That was all behind him. They both looked happy, healthy, and glad to be back on American soil.

Cue the music:
"Day after Day"
Badfinger

Many people believe that great leaders are born, not made. They have a native capacity in their personality that blossoms under pressure and makes others want to give them their allegiance. When the leader takes the wheel, the followers feel safe riding along.

Most any list of the world's greatest leaders would include Alexander III of Macedon, commonly known as Alexander the Great. Macedon was a large region of northern Greece without clearly defined borders. Alexander lived thirty-two short years from 356 BC to 323 BC, but he had an enormous impact on the world of that era and the world we know today.

Alexander was the child of Phillip II and Olympias, one of Phillip's seven wives. She claimed on the night before Alexander's birth to have dreamed that a lightning bolt had struck her womb. To Olympias, the lightning bolt signified a link to Zeus, king of the pantheon of Greek gods. Historians debate whether Olympias promoted the belief in Alexander's divine parentage by Zeus, or if she ever told her son the story.

Seeing potential in his growing son, Phillip began looking for a teacher. He made a bargain with Aristotle, renowned for his expansive knowledge, to teach Alexander and the children of his high ranking military officers. Phillip would rebuild Aristotle's hometown and free the citizens from slavery in exchange for him instructing the students.

Phillip provided the Temple of the Nymphs at Mieza as a private boarding school. Aristotle taught a well-rounded curriculum, including philosophy, religion, art, morality, and logic. The young Alexander became a passionate student of Homer, and later he carried his copy of the *Iliad* into battle.

Only in his teens, Alexander ascended to leadership when his father was assassinated. He sought to expand his father's conquests 'to the ends of the world and the Great Outer Sea'. In battle after battle for thirteen years, Alexander and his troops were never defeated. His dominion stretched from the Ionian Sea near where we lived in Greece all the way to India at the foot of the Himalayas. Alexander falsely believed that the world ended there.

Alexander's empire spread Hellenistic culture, foods, and ideas far and wide. Greeks were enabled to colonize a greatly expanded area beyond their country's borders. The soldiers carried olives, grapes, and chickpeas, and introduced them to the peoples they encountered. They brought back melons and oranges to Greece. Rice and exotic spices from India, and cinnamon and eggplant from Turkey were carried back. The sojourning troops learned the art of distilling spirits and liquors during their worldly conquests.

Using Athens as his ideal civic model, Alexander founded twenty cities, which all bore his name. The most significant, Alexandria, Egypt, was founded in 331 BC. For nearly one thousand years, Alexandria was the Mediterranean's busiest center of trade. The city contained the Library of Alexandria, a great repository of ancient knowledge. A government edict mandated that every foreign vessel entering the harbor had to turn over all their scrolls for copying. The copies were placed in the library.

Alexander's troops followed him unwaveringly in campaign after campaign, until they reached the Hydaspes River at the foot of the Himalayas, the world's tallest mountains. There they fought their last major conflict, the Battle of Hydaspes. Their adversary was the army of the Indian ruler, Porus, perhaps their most skilled opponent. Porus' forces included fierce war elephants. Despite the mayhem of soldiers being crushed and tossed in the air by tusks, Alexander's army prevailed. His men were war weary, however, and bone-tired after their 14,000 miles of conquest. With the daunting and treacherous mountain range awaiting them, the men refused to go any farther.

The general Coenus pleaded the troops' case with Alexander. He said they longed to see their parents, their wives, their children, and their homeland once again. Alexander finally agreed, and the army turned back toward the south. Alexander had a great vision, but those who carried it out were only human.

Alexander and his army returned to the city of Babylon in Persia, which is in present-day Iraq. He found those he had left in charge had misbehaved badly. He summarily executed several of those he had formerly trusted. Alexander tried many concessions to rally his troops again and win back their allegiance, but nothing worked.

In the end, I believe Alexander the Great was humbled by the smallest of adversaries, a bacterium. Historians have speculated whether foul play was involved in Alexander's early demise at age thirty-two. Since he developed a fever, and it took him two weeks to die, I agree with those who think a bacterial infection, malaria, or typhoid fever ended his life.

Just eight years after Alexandria, Egypt, was established, Alexander the Great's body was taken there for entombment by his trusted general, Ptolemy I Soter. The body was en route to Alexander's home region, Macedon, but Ptolemy waylaid it. The tradition said the succeeding ruler would bury his predecessor. Ptolemy was the Greek ruler of Egypt and was also a Roman citizen. He was vying for more territory to rule over.

Ptolemy loved Alexander. He had been with him since childhood and had been Alexander's trusted bodyguard. Some historians believe he may have been Alexander's half-brother. The tomb of Alexander became an early tourist destination for visitors from abroad. Its whereabouts are not known today.

Six hundred eighty-eight years later in the summer of 365 AD, the sea suddenly drained from Alexandria's busy harbor. Ships keeled over, and fish flailed on the sandy bottom of the dry harbor. People wandered out into the eerily empty expanse. Then suddenly, the huge wave of a tsunami rushed over them, tossing the ships like toys. Eye witnesses recorded their descriptions of the horrific scene. As many as fifty thousand people perished that day. The date is still commemorated today in modern Alexandria.

Cue the music:
"Homeward Bound"
Simon and Garfunkel

The Greek people take everything concerning the Olympics to heart. No matter where the modern Olympics take place, Greeks still feel a sort of ownership. After all, the Olympics were held on Greek soil for a thousand years before any other country participated in the games. The torch still originates in Olympia.

The 1972 Summer Olympics started on August 26th, and the events had been going on in Munich, Germany for ten days. We saw the Kato villagers huddled around televisions in cafés and a few stores, watching the striving athletes. Greece had sixty contestants competing in nine sports and forty-nine events that year.

On September 5, 1972, our American expatriate community noticed a distinct change in the people we encountered around Kato. They were distant and not the usual friendly neighbors we were so fond of. We could tell they were upset about something, but we weren't sure what it was.

Later that afternoon, one of the American wives who had

never visited our home before showed up on our doorstep. I could see she was extremely agitated.

"What happened?" I asked, fearing there had been an accident.

"The Greeks are throwing rocks at us. They threw them at me and my husband and at Jess," she said.

"Was anyone hurt?" I asked.

"No. They didn't hit us. They just scared us. But something isn't right."

"We'd better find out what's going on. I'll tell Al as soon as he gets here. Do you want to stay here until then?"

"No. The guys are on the corner waiting for me. I didn't want you or your kids to get hurt if you walked to town."

"Thank you," I said as I hugged her. "Thank you so much." I was sincerely touched that she had thought about my children's welfare.

The news of the rock throwing spread quickly, and it alarmed everyone. None of the Americans could understand what had changed so suddenly. We had to find out what was going on outside our little village.

We finally heard the news from the Summer Olympics in Munich that a Palestinian terrorist group called Black September had broken into the Olympic village. Two Israeli athletes had been murdered and eleven were being held hostage.

Security had been intentionally low key at the Olympic Village. Officials didn't want to draw any comparisons to the 1936 Berlin Olympics, which had been used by Nazi Adolph Hitler to fuel his propaganda machine. Athletes often came and went without showing their credentials. Some even took short cuts by climbing over the six-and-a-half-foot-tall chain link fence surrounding the apartments.

The eight terrorists were able to enter the village at 4:30 a.m. by climbing over the fence. They wore track suits and carried duffel bags full of weapons. They blended in. Some unsuspecting Canadian athletes even helped the Black September members over the fence.

Originally, the news reports said Americans had assisted the terrorists. I believe that report is what sparked the anger of our neighbors in Kato. The confusion wasn't cleared up until much later.

Once inside the apartment complex, the eight Palestinians used stolen keys to intrude on the sleeping Israelis. Many of the athletes were wrestlers and weight lifters, and they put up a lot of resistance. A wrestling coach and a weightlifter fought back bravely, but were quickly shot and killed. A few managed to escape, but the remaining nine hostages were subdued with assault rifles and pistols.

The Black September members demanded the release of 234 Palestinians jailed in Germany and punctuated their demand by throwing the wrestling coach's body outside the residence. The Israeli government's response was immediate. They would not negotiate with terrorists. The Munich police offered the kidnappers a large sum of money, but their offer was quickly rejected.

A small group of covert police officers dressed as athletes were able to get close to the crime scene, but camera crews filmed them and broadcast the images on television. The Black September members watched the whole operation on TV as the police took their positions. The threat to kill more hostages caused the police to give up and leave the area.

Negotiators arranged for the German Minister of the Interior and the mayor of the Olympic Village to be allowed to talk briefly with the hostages. The mayor later spoke of the dignity of the Israeli hostages and their resignation to certain death. He said many of the athletes looked as if they had been physically abused. He incorrectly reported to the police that there were only four or five Palestinians, which proved to be a fatal error. At around 6:00 p.m. the terrorists made a new demand for air transport to Cairo, Egypt.

The German negotiators feigned agreement, even though the Egyptian government had already said they wanted no involvement in the crisis. A bus was arranged to carry the hostages and their kidnappers to two military helicopters. From there, they would fly to Furstenfeldbruck, a NATO air force base, where the German authorities planned an armed ambush. Five snipers were positioned around the tarmac. Inside a Boeing 727 were six armed German police officers dressed as flight crew members.

When the transfer was made from the bus to the helicopters, the police realized there were eight terrorists instead of five. Plans were immediately changed, and the flight crew evacuated the 727. The helicopters landed at the air base at 10:30 p.m. Four of the Palestinians held the helicopter pilots at gunpoint, while two inspected the plane.

When they saw the plane was empty, they realized they had been lured into a trap. The two terrorists sprinted back to the helicopters. The snipers opened fire. Two of the kidnappers were killed, but the remaining gunmen scrambled to safety. The hostages were tied up inside the helicopters.

Around midnight, German armored personnel carriers arrived at the air base. Sensing they were losing the upper hand, at four minutes after midnight on September 6th one of the terrorists fired on the Israeli hostages point blank and then tossed a live grenade into the cockpit. The helicopter exploded, and the bound hostages were incinerated.

In the ensuing gunfire, all the remaining Israeli hostages in the second helicopter and three more of the terrorists died. The three remaining Black September members were taken into custody and imprisoned.

Many tactical errors contributed to the failure of the ambush. The snipers did not have radios, and their firearms were inadequate for the distance. The helicopters landed in a position that allowed the Palestinians to take cover behind them.

The bodies of five of the Black September members were flown to Libya, where they received full military honors.

Golda Meir, Prime Minister of Israel, secretly authorized the Israeli Intelligence Agency, Mossad, to hunt down and kill those responsible for the massacre. The mission became known as Operation Wrath of God.

We had already returned to America when Black September members skyjacked a Lufthansa 727 over Turkey on October 29, 1972. They demanded the release of the three remaining Palestinians still imprisoned in Germany awaiting trial. The terrorists were freed in order to rescue the Lufthansa passengers. Of the three Palestinians, two were hunted down and killed by Operation Wrath of God. One is believed to still be alive.

The sole positive aspect of the massacre was that it made countries worldwide recognize the looming threat of terrorism. They began establishing counter-terrorism measures. After September 5, 1972, Al and the other airmen at Araxos Detachment were ordered to carry loaded weapons at all times.

Our Greek neighbors seemed to be grieving for the Israeli athletes, but even more so for what had been done to the Olympic tradition. They didn't seem to blame us Americans anymore, and they were kind and friendly to us again. Though our relationships with the locals returned to normal, there remained a shroud of gloom over Kato.

Cue the music:
"What the World Needs Now is Love"
Jackie DeShannon

13 – RAMBLE ON

I love the balmy summer days and the perfect waves, but I love the change of the seasons, too. Every year toward the end of summer, I begin yearning to wear plaid and watch football games. I want to make stew and bake crusty bread. Pristine tablets, sharpened number two pencils, and the smell of erasers always signify a brand new start to me. Autumn has brought me new friends and new things to learn. Except for random continuing education classes, I haven't been to school in over forty years. No matter, I still get a back-to-school longing in the late summer.

In 1972, my longing was mixed with a craving to be in my own country. As much as I loved living in Greece, I was still eager to go home to the America I knew and to my family. I yearned to embrace my mother and father and tell them how much I missed them.

I think all expatriates feel this way at some point. There is an ease we feel when we're in our own hometown, in our own neighborhood, that can't be duplicated. We go out into the world searching for the treasure we have right there at home.

Al and I knew we would be leaving Kato on September 11, 1972, to start our journey back to the USA. I had our passport and the return part of our round-trip ticket ready for the kids and me. This trip, Al would be traveling with us, which would make things much easier for me. Matt wouldn't need to wear his leash . . . er child safety device.

A month before our departure, a new airman and his wife moved in with us. Al and the airman had made an arrangement. Al and I moved out of our bedroom, and the new airman and his wife moved in. The couple would take ownership of our

Peanut car, our house, and all our household goods when we left on September 11th. They were newlyweds without children, so Tammy's crib could be given to another family.

I wish I could say that our attempt at communal living went swimmingly, but that was not the case. The living arrangement made our last month in Greece seem to drag by, and we were all getting on each other's nerves by the day of our departure.

I learned that even beneficent bohemians have to draw a line in the sand sometimes. I was happy to share what we had, but I wasn't going to become their full-time maid, cook, and wash woman. They seemed to think of themselves as our house guests, rather than our roommates.

"These people are driving me crazy!" I vented to Al when he came home from the det.

"What did she do?" he asked, sensing that the wife was the one I had a problem with. The husband had been at the det all day, too.

"She left dirty clothes and wet towels strewn all over the bathroom and left a big mess in the kitchen. All she did was peel a piece of fruit, and it looks like she cooked a five course meal."

"It's only a few more days. Can you hang in there?"

"I guess I don't have a choice. This place is gonna look like a wreck a week after we're gone."

The gypsies visited our home for one last time, and we did some major bargaining. One gypsy woman, who was always beautifully dressed, had been coveting my full-length fake fur and pleather coat all during the cold season. I decided she would love wearing it more than I did, so I traded it to her for an embroidered tablecloth and a few other souvenirs. She tried it on and spun around in our kitchen, beaming with pride and happiness. My suitcase would be a little lighter on the way home.

The Air Force allowed us to ship one wooden crate home, so we loaded it with our orange Flokati rug, some miniature replicas of famous Greek statuary, a vase, the brass candlesticks we bought in Patras, our gypsy tablecloth, a fur Greek key rug, a decorated tile, my Retsina tankard from the winery, a donkey saddle, some worry beads, and a few clothes.

All the Americans bought donkey saddles to take home for some unknown reason. The donkey saddle business in Kato must have had a super salesman. The pack saddles, which were made of wood, were meant to be a framework for tying a heavy load onto the back of some hapless burro. The saddle maker burned a few designs and the words 'Kato Achaia' into the wood.

The saddle we shipped back sat around for years afterward in our rec room, totally ignored. We certainly didn't have a donkey to saddle up.

I'm not sure how the crate was shipped to the States, but it took months to arrive at our door. I suppose they waited for available space on a cargo plane. A few of the items arrived broken, but most survived the long trip.

We walked around Kato, visiting our neighbors and the local store keepers for the last time. We bid our landlord and his family, *"Adi'o,"* and *"Ef karisto,"* meaning 'goodbye' and 'thank you'. We could say no more in their language, but hoped our eyes conveyed our thoughts as we clasped their hands.

I had a little ache in my heart, leaving these kind people who had welcomed our family so warmly. I hoped then that we could return to Kato someday. We had lived gently there. Would they remember us?

I would like to take our family back to all the places we knew in Greece and duplicate the photos we snapped back in the 1970s. I especially want the family to sit together on that bench near the Acropolis. That plan is on my bucket list.

Cue the music:
"Two of Us (On Our Way Home)"
The Beatles

On our last day in Kato, a cab driver Al had gotten to know revealed a secret that had been kept from us for the entire year. He told us that we had been paying the electric bill for the well-lit bus station and the street light outside our home, included in our $43.00 monthly rent. Apparently, everyone in town knew this but us. We had a good laugh about it.

I was secretly glad. I hoped our contribution had made the life of our landlord and his family a little easier. We didn't tell the couple who had moved into our house. They weren't known for their generosity, so we kept the secret.

Al's last work day at the Araxos Detachment was marred by a tragedy. An American military policeman shot himself playing Russian roulette in the barracks. We had no idea what caused him to take this self-destructive risk. The last thing Al saw at the det was the MP's body lying in the back of a station wagon with his boots tied together. The car drove off, and Al left the Araxos Detachment right behind it, never to return.

Our closest American friends, Mac and Roberta, drove us to Athens in their vehicle. Their car was slightly larger than the Peanut. We loaded our single suitcase and Al's duffle bag into the trunk, said goodbye to the couple who had moved in with us, and piled into the car.

I had bittersweet feelings about leaving. I looked back for one last time at our stucco villa and our Peanut car. We sure had been happy there. But our future was wide open. In a few days, Al would be discharged from the Air Force, and we would be the masters of our own destiny for the first time in four years. We were excited about our plans to open a business in Colorado Springs.

During the four-hour trip, I tried to commit to memory everything we passed along the way. We stopped at the Corinth Canal Café for a frappé and a rest stop, as usual. The traffic gradually increased as we drove into the heart of Athens, ending up at our favorite hotel, The Kreoli, for one last night.

The luxuriously smooth marble floors and heavy cotton bed linens acted like tranquilizers on the whole family. We'd been there so many times that we felt at home. We knew the view from the balcony well.

That evening, we dined with our friends at a nearby restaurant. I had *moussaka* for my last Greek meal. We returned to our room to settle in for the night. We needed to be at the airport early the next day.

The tribe slept soundly. I awoke early in the morning before the rest of the family, anticipating all the things I needed to repack before departing for the airport. While they slept a little while longer, I went into the marble-clad bathroom to perform my morning ablutions.

I had just sat down on the porcelain 'throne' when the room started to move. It rocked and rolled, until I expected the marble tiles would start to pop off the walls. I was almost knocked off my polished white perch. My first thought was, *Oh, no. Don't let us die on the day we're supposed to go home to America!*

The earthquake seemed to last several minutes, but I know in reality it was really only seconds. It's odd how time seems to slow down in the middle of a disaster. I remember slipping off a small step ladder once. I seemed to watch myself fall in slow motion. What a strange sensation it is.

I burst from the bathroom, abruptly waking up the family. Al and the kids roused from their peaceful slumber. They had snoozed through the whole earthquake. Al looked skeptical when I told him what had happened.

Later, when we crossed through the lobby downstairs, we heard several people discussing the quake and whether aftershocks were expected. I felt like a baby bird being prodded to leave the nest. I couldn't get my family out of there fast enough.

We checked in at the airport, and with hugs and kisses we bid our friends farewell. The kids had changed a lot from the way they looked in our passport picture, but I wasn't worried. Anyone could tell they definitely belonged to us.

As eventful as our trip over to Greece had been, the reverse version was uneventful, except for the earthquake. We settled into our comfortable seats. Al was looking trim in his khaki uniform on one side of the aisle. The kids and I were directly across the aisle from him.

Matt and Tammy, the young but seasoned travelers, were happy to be going on a trip. For weeks, Al and I had talked up the fun of flying in a jet. One of the first phrases Matt learned to say was 'plane in the sky'. I think he understood we were going home to see his beloved grandparents, aunts, and uncles. Tammy was too young when we left the US to remember them, but it wouldn't take her long to get reacquainted.

We had a direct flight, which would take us to New York in several hours less time than the trip over had taken. We had smooth air for the entire flight. There were no storms, turbulence, or stops for fumigation along the way.

Our rustic village home had seemed a universe away from the United States, but in only a few hours we were transported back to our native land.

When the plane approached New York, and we felt the landing gear go down, a rush of elation and delight bubbled over in us. I reached across the aisle to Al. We clasped hands tightly and smiled broadly, like a couple of happy face bumper stickers. We were back where we belonged.

Cue the music:
"Spirit in the Sky"
Norman Greenbaum

Coda

My time on earth won't have the historical significance of Socrates or Alexander the Great, but I've lived a rich and fulfilling life. I believe God created me to be a wife and mother and gave me the skills I would need for the job. I'm sure He enabled me to meet the challenges of living in Kato with my little family. Our year abroad had happy times and sad times, but looking back, the tragedies have lost their sting. The joy and the love remain.

I've recreated what I can of Kato in my Texas backyard. My lemon tree will yield a large harvest around Thanksgiving. My olive tree is thriving, but hasn't produced a crop yet. I sit on my patio, sipping espresso and thinking I need to plant a grapevine over the arbor. I don't have any sheep, goats, or donkeys grazing on my lawn, but there are some just down the road.

I'm sixty-four years old now. Facing my own mortality, I sometimes think about what Heaven may bring. My perfect day in a perfect Heaven would be spent painting, listening to opera and rock and roll, while cooking for everyone I love. I would work in the soil in a garden and play with all the pets I've had in my lifetime. And then I would splash in the ocean surf. My perfect Heaven would be beautifully simple, and it would look just like Greece.

KALÍ ÓREKSI!
'ENJOY YOUR MEAL'

Lamb Souvlaki

Lamb shoulder, boned with most of the fat removed

1/3 cup extra virgin olive oil

Juice of 1 lemon

2 cloves garlic, crushed

1 teaspoon dried oregano, crushed

1 teaspoon dried thyme, crushed

Salt & pepper, to taste

Individual bamboo skewers, presoaked in water

Limes, quartered

1 crusty loaf of bread, cut lengthwise

2 - 3 tablespoons extra virgin olive oil for the bread

Slice the lamb into 1-inch cubes. Place 1/3 cup olive oil, the lemon juice, garlic, and herbs into a large ziplock bag. Add the lamb cubes. Place the sealed bag in the refrigerator for approximately 8 hours, turning occasionally.

Light the charcoal grill and place the grate 6 inches above the coals. While the charcoal gets ready, remove the meat cubes from the marinade, reserving the marinade. Place 5 or 6 lamb cubes on each presoaked skewer, leaving a small space between each cube. Place the prepared skewers on the hot charcoal grill. Brush each skewer with marinade. Grill 5 minutes. Turn the souvlaki over. Brush with marinade again. Finish grilling 5-7 minutes until the meat edges are browned.

Meanwhile, brush the cut side of the bread with 2-3 tablespoons of olive oil and toast it, cut side down on the grill. When golden, remove the bread from the grill and cut it into bite-sized cubes.

Immediately after removing the souvlaki from the grill, squeeze lime juice over them. Add a cube of bread to the end of each skewer. Add salt and pepper to taste.

Ω Ω Ω

Marinating meat in olive oil has been scientifically proved to virtually eliminate cancer-causing agents from grilling. The Greek diet is one of the healthiest on the planet.

I was sad to hear that pork has replaced lamb in most souvlakia served today in Greece. It may be more economical, but nothing can replace the hypnotic fragrance and flavor of the herbed lamb cooking over charcoal. The captivating aroma will draw the diners to your table.

Nescafé Frappé

2 teaspoons Nescafé Clásico Instant Coffee Powder

1/3 cup cold water

5 ice cubes

1-3 teaspoons sugar (or preferred sweetener), to taste

1/4 cup half and half cream and milk, to taste

Place the coffee powder and water in a cocktail shaker or a jar with a tight fitting lid. Shake until the mixture forms thick foam.

Place the ice cubes in a tall glass. Pour the coffee mixture over the ice. Add the sugar and half and half to taste. Serve with a straw.

Ω Ω Ω

The flavor of the frappé is the closest you can get to an iced espresso drink without owning an espresso machine. The Nestlé company based in Switzerland brought their instant coffee to stores and restaurants in 1938. In 1972, Nescafé had a strong market share in Greece. It was the only brand we saw being served, and the word Nescafé had replaced the word coffee, much as Coke has replaced soda in America. You may substitute another brand if you prefer.

Tzatziki Sauce

1 small cucumber, peeled and seeded

1 cup plain Greek yogurt

1 clove garlic, crushed

1 teaspoon extra virgin olive oil

1 tablespoon fresh mint leaves, minced

Salt, to taste at serving time

Prepare the sauce right before serving. Slice the peeled cucumber lengthwise. Use a melon baller to scoop the seeds from the cucumber. Grate the cucumber coarsely into a colander. Press the grated cucumber with paper towels to remove as much liquid as possible. Blend the drained cucumber into the yogurt. Add the garlic, oil, and minced mint leaves.

Do not add the salt until you are ready to serve. Adding salt earlier will cause the sauce to separate and get watery.

Ω Ω Ω

I use spearmint from my garden for this recipe. I don't think peppermint would be the right mint for this sauce. Tzatziki is a versatile and fresh tasting sauce that complements grilled seafood and meats, as well as fried appetizers.

Fried Fruit Pies

Pastry:

2 cups all-purpose flour

Pinch of salt

1 egg

4 tablespoons olive oil

2 tablespoons water

Combine the flour and salt in a medium-sized bowl. In a small bowl, beat the egg with a fork. Add the olive oil and water to the beaten egg. Blend until combined.

Make a well in the center of the flour. Add the wet mixture gradually, mixing it in with a fork until all the liquid is incorporated and the dough forms a ball. Put the dough in the refrigerator until well chilled. Meanwhile, make the filling.

Filling:

3 cups dried fruit of choice (I used peaches, apples, and plums)

1 cup water

1/3 cup sugar

1/2 teaspoon ground cinnamon

Cut the fruit into bite-sized pieces. Cover the fruit with the water in a saucepan. Add the sugar. Bring the mixture to a simmer for 30 to 45 minutes until the fruit is tender and the sauce is thickened. Watch closely toward the end of the cooking time to avoid scorching. Remove the saucepan from the heat and add the cinnamon. Stir gently. Allow to cool down to room temperature.

Assembling the pies:

Divide the dough into 4 balls. Leave 3 of the portions in the refrigerator. Roll out one ball of dough on a floured surface. Work in enough flour to make the dough easy to handle. Don't be concerned if you have to add quite a bit of flour. Fried pie dough is not as delicate as regular pie crust. Use a 6-inch saucer as a template to cut a circle of dough. Place the dough circles on a tray that has been covered with parchment or waxed paper. Roll out the remaining refrigerated portions, one by one, and cut out circles until all the dough is used.

Spoon 2 rounded tablespoons of filling in the center of each dough circle. Dampen the edges of the dough lightly with water. Fold half of the circle over the other half. Crimp the dough edges by folding them over and pinching them. The tines of a fork may also be used for crimping the edges. These pies are rustic, and they don't look perfect. The important thing is to make sure the dough is sealed, so the filling stays inside.

Frying the pies:

In a large skillet, pour oil to a depth of approximately 1 inch. Heat the oil up to frying temperature, approximately 350 degrees Fahrenheit. The oil should be hot, but not smoking. Test by frying a small scrap of dough. When the oil is ready, slide a spatula under each pie and lift them into the hot oil. Don't fry more than 3 at once.

Add more oil when necessary. Watch the pies carefully. Lift an edge to see if the dough has browned. Then gently turn the pie over in the oil, using two spatulas. When the pies are golden brown on both sides, remove them to drain on paper towels. Sugar may be sprinkled on the finished pies. Continue until all the pies are fried.

Ω Ω Ω

These fried pies have absolutely no resemblance to the ones served by fast food restaurants in America. These are simple countrified comfort food. They taste great warm or cold. You might not think it is possible to make pastry dough without butter, lard, or shortening, but it is. Olive oil makes silky-smooth dough which can be rolled out thin, and it is healthier for your family.

When substituting olive oil for butter or margarine, use less. For instance, 3/4 cup of olive oil substitutes for 1 cup of butter. In Kato, olive oil was used to make layered filo dough. I never saw any butter for sale in our local stores.

While in Greece, I used only what was available locally. I didn't have paper towels, so I drained the pies on layers of newspaper covered with clean kitchen towels.

The pie filling options we have in the USA are endless. There are so many fresh, frozen, and dried fruits to choose from. Interesting combinations of fruits, nuts, and puddings make good fillings. I especially like apples and cranberries with pecans.

In the southern part of America known as 'Dixie', they call these desserts 'hand pies' and fry them in a black cast iron skillet. Be adventurous. You might create something wonderful.

Fried Okra

A 'mess' of fresh okra (it will take more than you think)

Corn meal

Flour

1 egg, beaten

Oil

1 tablespoon bacon grease

Salt & pepper, to taste

Wash and drain the okra. Remove and discard the stem ends and tips. Cut the okra pods crosswise into 1/2-inch sections. Place the okra pieces in a large bowl. Pour the beaten egg over the okra and toss to coat all the pieces. Combine equal parts flour and corn meal in a bowl. Sprinkle the flour and corn meal mixture over the okra pieces. Toss to coat. Allow to stand for 1/2 hour.

Then pour the coated okra pieces into a colander. Shake gently to remove excess flour and corn meal.

Pour the oil into a large skillet to a depth of 1/2 inch. Add the tablespoon of bacon grease to the oil. More bacon grease may be used if you prefer. Heat the oil to frying temperature, approximately 350 degrees Fahrenheit. The oil should be hot, but not smoking. Test the temperature with one piece of okra. When the oil is ready, add the breaded okra pieces all at once. Turn the pieces over to coat all of them with oil. Then leave the pieces in place until the first side is browned. Turn all the browned pieces once using a spatula. Fry the second side until browned. Remove the okra when it is nicely golden on all sides. Drain the okra on paper towels. Add salt and pepper to taste.

Ω Ω Ω

Frying is not my favorite cooking method, but I had to employ it in Greece to add a variety of tastes and textures to our meals. Since I only had a three burner hot plate and no oven, stewing, steaming, and boiling got to be tiresome.

Fried okra is a quintessential Southern American side dish. In Greece, we sometimes made it our main dish. It was delicious with sliced fresh tomatoes on the side.

Avgolemono
(Egg Lemon Soup)

4 cups chicken broth

1/3 cup long grain rice

3 egg yolks

1 large lemon, juiced

2 tablespoons fresh parsley

Salt & pepper, to taste

Bring the broth to a simmer in a large pot. Add the rice. Cover and simmer 15 minutes until the rice is tender. Remove the pot from the burner.

In a bowl, whisk the egg yolks. Add the lemon juice to the yolks, whisking constantly until bubbles form. Add a ladle of the hot broth slowly to the egg mixture while whisking constantly. This will temper the egg mixture to avoid curdling.

Add the tempered egg mixture to the broth slowly, while whisking constantly. The soup will thicken slightly. Stir in the fresh parsley. Serve immediately. Serves four.

ΩΩΩ

For a Texas twist on this soup recipe, I add fresh cilantro in place of the parsley. In Texas, not every grocery store has fresh parsley, but they all have fresh cilantro for making salsa. Simply wash the cilantro and strip the leaves from the stems. There is no need to chop the herbs. Avgolemono is a summery soup. The color is pale lemon yellow contrasting with the green herb leaves. It makes a lovely lunch dish with a sandwich or salad.

Keik Siropi Lemonati
(Lemony Syrup Cake)

Cake:

2 cups self-rising flour

2 teaspoon baking powder

1 cup sugar

1/2 cup butter, at room temperature

1 cup thick Greek yogurt

4 eggs

Zest of 2 large lemons (or 3 small lemons)

2 tablespoons lemon juice

Syrup Glaze:

Remaining juice of the 2 lemons listed above

Juice of 1 lime

Zest of 1 lime

1/2 cup powdered sugar

Preheat the oven to 350 degrees F/ 180 C. Line the bottom of a round 9-inch cake pan with parchment paper. Grease the sides of the pan. Set aside.

Place all the cake ingredients into a large mixing bowl. Using an electric mixer, combine the mixture until it forms a thick batter. Beat the batter for 2 minutes, scraping the sides of the bowl frequently.

Pour the batter into the prepared pan. Smooth out the surface. Bake for 60 minutes at 350 degrees F/ 180 C. Test the center with a toothpick. When it comes out clean, the cake is done.

While the cake is baking, prepare the syrup glaze by combining the remaining lemon juice, the lime juice and zest, and the 1/2 cup powdered sugar in a small saucepan. While stirring constantly, bring the mixture to a boil. Lower the heat and simmer the syrup glaze for about 3 minutes while continuing to stir. Set the glaze aside until the cake is finished baking.

As soon as the cake tests done, remove the pan from the oven. Run a knife around the edge to release the cake. Choose a serving plate with a lip to contain any glaze that doesn't soak into the cake. Pierce the top of the cake about one inch apart with a thin skewer. Slowly spoon about half the warm syrup glaze over the perforations in the warm cake.

Then turn the cake out of the pan onto the serving plate. The bottom side will remain up. Remove the parchment paper. Pierce the bottom of the cake as you did the top. Spoon the remaining syrup glaze over the perforations.

ΩΩΩ

Most Greek cakes are dense and moist with a texture like corn bread. *Keik siropi lemonati* is for lemon-lovers like me. It is delicious served warm and even better the second day after baking. The tangy flavors blend beautifully. My favorite espresso drink, an Americano, complements this cake.

Many European recipes call for self-rising flour, which they call 'self-raising'. Most American cake recipes say to combine the dry ingredients and set them aside, cream the butter, eggs, and sugar, and then add the dry ingredients to the creamed mixture. This Greek recipe streamlines those steps, so the cake batter is quickly prepared. When zesting the citrus, use a zesting tool or a very fine grater. Avoid getting the white pith into the batter. It makes the batter bitter!

Dolmades
(Stuffed Grape Leaves)

20 grape leaves (also known as vine leaves), washed

2 tablespoons olive oil

1 small onion, chopped finely

1/4 cup pine nuts

1 clove garlic, crushed

1/2 cup long grain rice, uncooked

1/4 teaspoon ground cinnamon

1 tablespoon fresh mint leaves, chopped

1/2 teaspoon salt

1/4 teaspoon pepper

2 cups chicken broth, divided

Olive oil for drizzle

Using tongs, plunge the grape leaves into boiling water a few at a time, for 3 or 4 seconds. This will darken them and make them flexible. Trim the stems from the leaves. Allow the leaves to drain while you prepare the filling.

In a skillet, sauté the chopped onion in the olive oil until soft and slightly browned. Add the pine nuts and garlic. Sauté the mixture for 3 minutes. Then add the uncooked rice, cinnamon, mint, salt, and pepper. Add 1/2 cup chicken broth.

Combine and simmer, covered, at low temperature for 10 minutes. Remove the skillet from the burner and allow the mixture to cool. The rice should be only partially cooked at this point.

The assembled dolmades may be cooked on the stove top in a large pot, or in the oven in a baking dish. The dolmades should fill the pan or dish in order to hold their shape. Line the bottom of your cooking vessel with 7 of the prepared leaves.

Pat the remaining leaves dry. Place 1 leaf, veins up on your work surface. Spoon about 1 tablespoon of the rice mixture an inch from the stem end of the leaf. Bring the stem end up and fold it over the filling. Fold in the left and right sides of the leaf. Then continue to roll toward the tip of the leaf forming an egg roll shape. The rolls should have a little room for expansion. Place each roll on the leaves in the prepared pan or dish, seam side down. Lay them side by side, closely, until all the rest of the leaves are filled. Pour the remaining 1 1/2 cups chicken broth gently over the dolmades in the pan.

Cover the pan or dish. If using the stove top, simmer at low temperature for 1 hour without lifting the lid. If baking, place the dish in an unheated oven. Set the temperature to 400 degrees F/ 205 C and bake for 30 minutes. Then lower the temperature to 325 degrees F/163 C for 30 more minutes. Bake without lifting the lid.

The dolmades may be served hot or chilled. Drizzle olive oil over the dolmades before serving.

Ω Ω Ω

Greek cooks sometimes add fish or ground lamb to the filling.

Authentic Greek Yogurt
(No special machine required)

Ingredients:

1/2 gallon milk, of your preference. The higher the fat content, the richer and thicker the yogurt will be.

2 heaping tablespoons of plain store-bought yogurt with active culture. This is your starter. After your first batch, you won't need to purchase any more yogurt. You will save a little from your batch to use as starter for the next batch.

Optional Additions:

2-3 tablespoons vanilla (for the batch)

Fruit, fresh, frozen, or puree

Sweetener of choice

Jam, jelly, or preserves

Powdered drink or cocoa mix, to taste

Instant coffee powder, to taste

Equipment you will need:

1 saucepan, 3-quart or larger, preferably with a pouring spout
1 cooking thermometer that registers 110 degrees Fahrenheit or 43 degrees Centigrade

10 canning jars, 8-ounce size

10 sets of canning lids and rings to fit the jars

1 strainer

1 electric heating pad (like you use for a sore back)

1 wire rack slightly larger than the heating pad

1 baking dish that will hold all 10 jars (I use 9"x12" Corningware or Pyrex)

1 dome-shaped bowl or pan large enough to place over the baking dish, rack, and heating pad. (This makes a canopy to hold in the heat.) A disposable foil roasting pan will work, but may lose some heat, so cooking time may need to be extended.

In the 3-quart or larger saucepan, bring the 1/2 gallon of milk to a boil. As soon as the milk begins to boil, remove the pan from the heat. A skin of cream may form on the top. Stir it back into the milk with a whisk. If using the vanilla, coffee, or cocoa mix, stir it into the batch at this point.

Place the 2 heaping tablespoons of store-bought yogurt in a small heat-proof dish.

Attach the thermometer to the pan. When the milk cools down to 110 degrees F/ 43 C, take a tablespoon of the hot milk from the pan and add it to the 2 tablespoons store-bought yogurt, stirring well. Then pour the yogurt mixture into the pan of hot milk. Whisk to combine thoroughly. Make sure the temperature is at 110 degrees F/ 43 C or slightly below, or the active culture will die.

Lay the heating pad on a heat-proof counter. Plug in the heating pad and set the dial to medium. Place the wire rack over the heating pad. Place the baking dish on the wire rack. Place the 10 open jars in the baking dish. Set the lids and rings nearby.

Pour the milk and yogurt mixture into the 10 jars through a small strainer to remove any lumps that may have formed. Position the overturned large bowl or foil pan over the baking dish and the open jars. The cover shouldn't fit flush to the counter. It needs to make a canopy to hold in the heat with an inch of space left for evaporation. You may devise a spacer to raise the canopy slightly off the counter if needed.

Set a timer for 10 hours.

At the end of the cooking time, remove the cover. The yogurt should be set and the consistency of pudding. If not thick enough, cook the yogurt longer, keeping in mind that the cooled yogurt will thicken slightly. Two or three hours more cooking time won t harm the yogurt.

When the yogurt is done, place a lid and ring on each jar and refrigerate them.

Tamara's Pumpkin Spice Yogurt

1 can pumpkin puree, 15-ounce size

1 teaspoon ground cinnamon

1/4 teaspoon ground nutmeg

1/4 teaspoon ground allspice

Follow the basic yogurt directions, but use 2 cups less milk. After adding the yogurt starter, stir in the canned pumpkin puree, cinnamon, nutmeg, and allspice.

Pour the mixture into the jars and cook as usual.

Ω Ω Ω

As the Pumpkin Spice Yogurt cooks, it will form lovely layers with the pumpkin on the bottom. It is a healthy and delicious alternative to pumpkin pie.

Ω Ω Ω

The difference in Greek yogurt and ordinary yogurt is the whey content. Whey is the clear watery substance that forms when the milk separates when heated. The Greek yogurt whey has been either strained off or evaporated. My recipe uses evaporation to achieve the thick and creamy product.

The yogurt cream cheese recipe below employs straining in cheesecloth to remove more of the whey.

The individual jars of yogurt are perfect for packing in a lunch. There is just enough space at the top to add your favorite fruit or flavoring. Add frozen berries and a stevia packet in the morning as you pack your lunch. By noon, the berries will be thawed and can be mixed into the yogurt.

This yogurt is the real thing. It is pure, simple, unadulterated, and economical. It contains no added sugar, salt, or gelatin. The only sugar in it is the lactose found naturally in milk.

Eating yogurt is a much better way to get your calcium and B vitamins than popping a pill. The nutrients are absorbed slowly as the yogurt moves through the digestive tract. Active culture yogurt is an excellent source of healthy probiotic bacteria, which aids digestion and boosts natural immunities. Regular consumption has been proved to lower the harmful LDL cholesterol.

Whole full-fat milk makes the creamiest yogurt.

Researchers have recently discovered that dairy fat is expelled from the body at a higher rate than other fats.

In Kato, the yogurt was made from sheep's milk. It was sweetened with honey for breakfast, used as a topping for vegetables, and added to soups as a thickener. Shepherds drank yogurt thinned with milk.

You can make your own 'pearl' of yogurt cream cheese by encasing 2 cups of thick yogurt in a square of layered cheesecloth. Tie up the corners and attach the 'pearl' to an upper kitchen cabinet handle. Suspend it there over a bowl for 2 to 3 days. The whey will drain into the bowl. The result is healthy cream cheese which can be used just like traditional cream cheese in recipes.

For a scrumptious appetizer, roll the cheese into bite-sized balls. Place them in a jar. Sprinkle your favorite herbs or peppers over the cheese balls. Pour extra virgin olive oil over the balls to cover. Store the cheese balls in the refrigerator up to three weeks. Serve with pita, flat bread, or crackers.

Store-bought yogurts have strayed far from the healthy path on which they started. Those labeled 'heat treated after culturing' will have fewer beneficial probiotics. Check out the added sugar content and the list of unpronounceable additives in the grocery store versions. Some contain more sugar than pudding does!

Once your taste buds get used to real Greek yogurt, you will recognize the delicious difference. I like it better than ice cream.